TANNISHŌ: PASSAGES DEPLORING DEVIATIONS OF FAITH

RENNYO SHŌNIN OFUMI: THE LETTERS OF RENNYO

BDK English Tripiṭaka Series

TANNISHŌ: PASSAGES DEPLORING DEVIATIONS OF FAITH

by

Yuienbō

Translated from the Japanese
(Taishō Volume 83, Number 2661)

by

Shōjun Bandō
in collaboration with Harold Stewart

RENNYO SHŌNIN OFUMI: THE LETTERS OF RENNYO

Translated from the Japanese
(Taishō Volume 74, Number 2668)

by

Ann T. Rogers and Minor L. Rogers

Bukkyō Dendō Kyōkai America, Inc.
1996

Second Printing, 2016
ISBN: 978-1-886439-03-0
Library of Congress Catalog Card Number: 95073152

Published by
BDK America, Inc.
1675 School Street
Moraga, California 94553

Printed in the United States of America

A Message on the Publication of the English Tripiṭaka

The Buddhist canon is said to contain eighty-four thousand different teachings. I believe that this is because the Buddha's basic approach was to prescribe a different treatment for every spiritual ailment, much as a doctor prescribes a different medicine for every medical ailment. Thus his teachings were always appropriate for the particular suffering individual and for the time at which the teaching was given, and over the ages not one of his prescriptions has failed to relieve the suffering to which it was addressed.

Ever since the Buddha's Great Demise over twenty-five hundred years ago, his message of wisdom and compassion has spread throughout the world. Yet no one has ever attempted to translate the entire Buddhist canon into English throughout the history of Japan. It is my greatest wish to see this done and to make the translations available to the many English-speaking people who have never had the opportunity to learn about the Buddha's teachings.

Of course, it would be impossible to translate all of the Buddha's eighty-four thousand teachings in a few years. I have, therefore, had one hundred thirty-nine of the scriptural texts in the prodigious Taishō edition of the Chinese Buddhist canon selected for inclusion in the First Series of this translation project.

It is in the nature of this undertaking that the results are bound to be criticized. Nonetheless, I am convinced that unless someone takes it upon himself or herself to initiate this project, it will never be done. At the same time, I hope that an improved, revised edition will appear in the future.

It is most gratifying that, thanks to the efforts of more than a hundred Buddhist scholars from the East and the West, this monumental project has finally gotten off the ground. May the rays of the Wisdom of the Compassionate One reach each and every person in the world.

NUMATA Yehan
Founder of the English
Tripiṭaka Project

August 7, 1991

Editorial Foreword

In January 1982, Dr. NUMATA Yehan, the founder of Bukkyō Dendō Kyōkai (Society for the Promotion of Buddhism), decided to begin the monumental task of translating the complete Taishō edition of the Chinese Tripiṭaka (Buddhist canon) into the English language. Under his leadership, a special preparatory committee was organized in April 1982. By July of the same year, the Translation Committee of the English Tripiṭaka was officially convened.

The initial Committee consisted of the following members: HANAYAMA Shōyū (Chairperson), BANDŌ Shōjun, ISHIGAMI Zennō, KAMATA Shigeo, KANAOKA Shūyū, MAYEDA Sengaku, NARA Yasuaki, SAYEKI Shinkō, (late) SHIOIRI Ryōtatsu, TAMARU Noriyoshi, (late) TAMURA Kwansei, URYŪZU Ryūshin, and YUYAMA Akira. Assistant members of the Committee were as follows: KANAZAWA Atsushi, WATANABE Shōgo, Rolf Giebel of New Zealand, and Rudy Smet of Belgium.

After holding planning meetings on a monthly basis, the Committee selected one hundred and thirty-nine texts for the First Series of translations, an estimated one hundred printed volumes in all. The texts selected are not necessarily limited to those originally written in India but also include works written or composed in China and Japan. While the publication of the First Series proceeds, the texts for the Second Series will be selected from among the remaining works; this process will continue until all the texts, in Japanese as well as in Chinese, have been published.

Frankly speaking, it will take perhaps one hundred years or more to accomplish the English translation of the complete Chinese and Japanese texts, for they consist of thousands of works. Nevertheless, as Dr. NUMATA wished, it is the sincere hope of the Committee that this project will continue unto completion, even after all its present members have passed away.

It must be mentioned here that the final object of this project is not academic fulfillment but the transmission of the teaching of the Buddha to the whole world in order to create harmony and peace among humankind. Therefore, any notes, such as footnotes and endnotes, which might be indispensable for academic purposes, are not given in the English translations, since they might make the general reader lose interest in the Buddhist scriptures. Instead, a glossary is added at the end of each work, in accordance with the translator's wish.

To my great regret, however, Dr. NUMATA passed away on May 5, 1994, at the age of ninety-seven, entrusting his son, Mr. NUMATA Toshihide, with the continuation and completion of the Translation Project. The Committee also lost its able and devoted Chairperson, Professor HANAYAMA Shōyū, on June 16, 1995, at the age of sixty-three. After these severe blows, the Committee elected me, Vice President of Musashino Women's College, to be the Chair in October 1995. The Committee has renewed its determination to carry out the noble intention of Dr. NUMATA, under the leadership of Mr. NUMATA Toshihide.

The present members of the Committee are MAYEDA Sengaku (Chairperson), BANDŌ Shōjun, ISHIGAMI Zennō, ICHISHIMA Shōshin, KAMATA Shigeo, KANAOKA Shūyū, NARA Yasuaki, SAYEKI Shinkō, TAMARU Noriyoshi, URYŪZU Ryūshin, and YUYAMA Akira. Assistant members are WATANABE Shōgo and MINOWA Kenryō.

The Numata Center for Buddhist Translation and Research was established in November 1984, in Berkeley, California, U.S.A., to assist in the publication of the BDK English Tripiṭaka First Series. In December 1991 the Publication Committee was organized at the Numata Center, with Professor Philip Yampolsky as the Chairperson. The Numata Center has thus far published seven volumes and has been distributing them. All of the remaining texts will be published under the supervision of this Committee, in close cooperation with the Translation Committee in Tokyo.

MAYEDA Sengaku
Chairperson
Translation Committee of
the BDK English Tripiṭaka

November 1, 1995

Publisher's Foreword

In December 1991, at the Numata Center for Buddhist Translation and Research in Berkeley, California, a publication committee was established for the purpose of seeing into print the translations of the Buddhist works in the BDK English Tripiṭaka Series. This committee processes the translations forwarded by the Translation Committee in Tokyo. It performs the duties of copyediting, formatting, proofreading, indexing, consulting with the translators on questionable passages, and so on—the routine duties of any publishing house. No attempt is made to standardize the English translations of Buddhist technical terms; these are left to the discretion of the individual translator. Represented on the committee are specialists in Sanskrit, Chinese, and Japanese, who attempt to ensure that fidelity to the texts is maintained.

This Publication Committee is dedicated to the production of lucid and readable works that do justice to the vision of the late Dr. NUMATA Yehan, who wished to make available to Western readers the major works of the Chinese and Japanese Buddhist canon.

"Taishō" refers to the *Taishō Shinshū Daizōkyō* (Newly Revised Tripiṭaka Inaugurated in the Taishō Era), which was published during the period from 1924 to 1934. This consists of one hundred volumes, in which as many as 3,360 scriptures in both Chinese and Japanese are included. This edition is acknowledged to be the most complete Tripiṭaka of the Northern tradition of Buddhism ever published in the Chinese and Japanese languages. As with all books in the BDK Series, the series number on the spine and title page of each work corresponds to the number ssigned to it by the Translation Committee of the BDK English Tripiṭaka in Tokyo. A list of the volume numbers is appended at the end of each volume. For the convenience of scholars who may wish to turn to the original texts, Taishō page and column numbers are provided in the margins of each volumes.

Those participating in the work of this committee are Diane Ames, Brian Galloway, Nobuo Haneda, Charles Niimi, and Rev. Kiyoshi S. Yamashita.

Philip Yampolsky
Chairperson
July 1, 1996   Publication Committee

ix

Contents

TANNISHŌ
PASSAGES DEPLORING DEVIATIONS OF FAITH

Contents

Translators' Introduction

Of the three canonical scriptures of the Pure Land schools, the *Larger Sutra* is the first mentioned in Japanese historical documents. Early references to this sutra appear in the writings of Shōtoku Taishi (574–622), and lectures on it were delivered at the Imperial court in 640 and 652 by the Japanese monk Eon. The remaining two Pure Land scriptures, the *Contemplation Sutra* and the *Smaller Sutra,* first appear in the records of the Shōsōin dating from the Nara period (710–793). The calling of the nenbutsu, the sacred Name of Amida Buddha (Amitābha), was introduced into Japan by Ennin (Jikaku Daishi, 794–864) after his return from study in China, but it was still combined with other meditational and ritual practices of the Tendai school. Later, during the Heian period (794–1185), Kūya Shōnin (903–972) popularized the nenbutsu among the common people of Kyoto, while Genshin (Eshin, 942–1017), by compiling the *Ōjōyōshū* (*Essentials of Rebirth*), was responsible for widening its influence throughout the country. At the beginning of the Kamakura period (1192–1333), Hōnen Shōnin (Genkū, 1133–1212) founded a separate Pure Land sect, the Jōdoshū, and preached sole reliance on the calling of Amida's Name. Finally, Shinran Shōnin (1173–1262), by placing the emphasis on faith transferred by Amida to the devotee, brought the development of Pure Land Buddhism in Japan to its consummation.

Although he refused to recognize any disciples, Shinran had, in fact, many ardent followers, including Yuienbō, the author of the *Tannishō*. Yuienbō was born at some date unknown to us and lived in Kawada, northeast of present-day Tokyo. He died in 1289, twenty-seven years after the death of Shinran. The *Tannishō* was probably written about 1280. Yuienbō's reason for writing the tract is given in the text itself: to refute deviations from the true faith that had arisen among Shin followers after Shinran's death.

The *Tannishō* has continued to exert a profound influence on Japanese life and thought ever since it was written. In the Muromachi period (1333–1573), Rennyo Shōnin (1415–1499), the eighth patriarch of the Honganji, who is regarded as the renewer of the Shinshū, added the following postscript to the *Tannishō:*

> This sacred scripture is one of the most valuable texts of our school. Those insufficiently matured in faith should not be allowed indiscriminately to read it.

In the Tokugawa period (1603–1868), Myō-on-in Ryōshō (1788–1842) made a special study of it, while in the Meiji period (1868–1912) it was a source of inspiration to Kiyozawa Manshi (1863–1903), a Shin Buddhist thinker. Since then its influence has spread to other Buddhist schools, including Zen. The famous philosopher Nishida Kitarō (1870–1945) said that if only two books were left in the world "it would be enough for me if I had only Shinran's *Tannishō* and the *Records of Rinzai.*" (He called it "Shinran's *Tannishō*" because so much of the work are direct quotes from Shinran.)

The book is organized into two parts, each preceded by a Foreword; an Afterword completes the text. The Afterword comprises three sections in which Yuienbō again quotes from Shinran, Hōnen, and Shandao (Zendō; 613–681), and to this was later added the postscript by Rennyo Shōnin quoted above.

The first part of the book, from the opening to the tenth passage, consists of Yuienbō's personal recollections of the words of Shinran himself, as received directly from the Master. The second part, from the eleventh to eighteenth passages, gives Yuienbō's own refutation of the deviations of faith that had arisen after Shinran's death, quoting in support of his argument further sayings of the Master. Following the Afterword but before the Postscript is an Appendix that gives details of the wrongful punishment and exile of Hōnen, Shinran, and other followers. As it is of great historical and biographical interest and importance, this section has also been translated here.

TANNISHŌ:
PASSAGES DEPLORING DEVIATIONS OF FAITH

Foreword

When I reflect with deep humility upon the past and the present, I cannot help 728a but deplore the prevalence of various deviations from the true faith transmitted by word of mouth from our late Master. So I feel concerned about possible doubts that may arise in the minds of future inheritors of the faith. Unless guided by a karmically related teacher, how could anyone expect to enter the gate of easy practice? Nobody should defile the doctrine of the other-power by his own arbitrary interpretations. Therefore I have recorded here the gist of what the late Shinran Shōnin told me, while it still reverberates in my ears. This has been written solely to clear away in advance any uncertainties that might arise among fellow devotees. So much by way of foreword.

I

"At the very moment when we are moved to utter the nenbutsu by a firm faith that our rebirth in the Pure Land is attained solely by virtue of the unfathomable working of Amida's Original Vow, we are enabled to share in its benefits that embrace all and forsake none. We should realize that Amida's Original Vow never discriminates between the old and the young, the good and the evil, and that what matters most is the heart of faith alone; for the vow 728b was originally made for the purpose of delivering sentient beings sorely defiled by their vices and passions. Therefore once faith in the Original Vow is steadfast, no other good is needed, for there is no good superior to the nenbutsu. No evil should be feared, for there is no evil powerful enough to obstruct Amida's Original Vow."

II

"Your earnest aim in coming all the way here to see me, crossing more than ten provinces at the risk of your lives, is solely to enquire of me the way to rebirth in the Land of Utmost Bliss. Nevertheless, should you honor me by supposing that I am withholding any esoteric way for rebirth in the Pure Land or that I know of scriptural sources other than the nenbutsu, you go seriously astray. Should you harbor such ideas, then there are a number of authoritative scholars in Nara, the Southern Capital, as well as on Mount Hiei, the Northern

Peak, whom you should visit and ask to your heart's content about the essentials for rebirth in the Pure Land.

"For me, Shinran, there is no alternative but to accept and trust in the teaching of my master Hōnen: that simply by uttering the nenbutsu I shall be given deliverance by Amida. Is the nenbutsu really the seed of rebirth in the Pure Land, or is it a karmic cause of falling into the lowest hell? Of such questions I know absolutely nothing. Even if I had been deceived by my master, Hōnen Shōnin, and were to fall into hellish torment, I would have no regrets at all! The reason is that, had I been one who was certain to attain buddhahood by striving at some other spiritual discipline and yet fell into an infernal state (i.e., hell) through uttering the nenbutsu, I might well be justified in regretting that I had been deceived. But as I find myself totally incapable of any kind of meritorious deed, the lowest hell would in any event be my destined abode.

728c

"If Amida's Original Vow is unfailing, then Śākyamuni's teaching cannot be false. If Śākyamuni's teaching is true, then Shandao's sacred commentaries cannot be unfounded. If Shandao's commentaries are well founded, how can Hōnen Shōnin's sayings be in error? If Hōnen Shōnin's sayings are trustworthy, how then can what I, Shinran, am telling you be in vain? Summing up, such are the humble convictions of my ignorant self. Beyond this, it depends entirely on each of you as to whether you adopt and trust in the nenbutsu or cast it aside."

III

"'Even a virtuous person can attain rebirth in the Pure Land, how much more easily a wicked person!' But ordinary people usually say: 'Even a wicked person can attain rebirth in the Pure Land, how much more easily a virtuous person.' At first sight, this view may appear more reasonable, but it really is quite contrary to the intention of the other-power of the Original Vow. The reason is that since a person who does deeds of merit by his own effort lacks total reliance on other-power, he is self-excluded from Amida's Original Vow. But as soon as his attitude of self-effort is redirected and he dedicates himself exclusively to the other-power, his rebirth in the true Land of Reward is at once assured.

"It was solely to enable the wicked to attain buddhahood that Amida took his vows, out of compassion for those like us who, defiled to the core, have no hope of liberating ourselves from the cycle of birth and death through any other discipline. And so an evil person who dedicates himself to the other-power is above all endowed with the right cause for rebirth. Hence Shinran's saying: 'Even a virtuous person can attain rebirth in the Pure Land, how much more easily a wicked person!'"

729a

IV

"There is a divergence between the compassion of the path of sages and that of the path of the Pure Land. The compassion of the path of sages commiserates with and cares for sentient beings, and yet it is least likely to succeed in liberating them as completely as could be wished. But the true compassion of the Pure Land path consists in calling the nenbutsu, thereby quickly attaining buddhahood, and then benefiting all sentient beings with the heart of great compassion and kindness as fully as possible. Because, as you know, no matter how much sympathy and pity we may feel for others in this life it is difficult to save them, as we would wish; our compassion is not thoroughgoing. And so the calling of the nenbutsu is the only all-embracing expression of the heart of great compassion."

V

"I, Shinran, have never called the nenbutsu, not even once, out of filial piety for my deceased parents. The reason is that through karmic relations during numberless rebirths, all sentient beings are or have been my parents or kinsmen. So we should attain buddhahood in the next life and then we shall be able to bring deliverance to all other beings.

"If the nenbutsu were a deed of merit that could be done by our own efforts, we could deliver our parents by transferring that merit to them. But this being impossible, only if we abandon our self-efforts and straightaway attain enlightenment in the Pure Land will Amida Buddha's superhuman powers and skillful means enable us to deliver first of all those with whom we are closely related by karmic ties, but who find themselves afflicted by suffering in any of the six realms of existence and the four modes of birth."

become a Buddha

11

VI

"It is unbelievable that any dispute should have arisen among those who devote themselves to the exclusive practice of the nenbutsu as to who are my disciples and who are the disciples of others. I, Shinran, do not have a single disciple of my own. The reason is that if I could induce others to call the nenbutsu through my own influence, then they might well be called my disciples. But it is utterly absurd to call them my disciples when they repeat the nenbutsu through the influence of Amida Buddha.

729b

"When karmic conditions are favorable, master and disciple must meet: when adverse, they must part. Despite this, there are those who disconcert the faithful by saying that if they desert their present master and repeat the nenbutsu while following some other master, their rebirth in the Pure Land can never be attained. At this, words fail me. Do they mean that they wish to revoke the faith called forth by Amida Buddha, as though it were their own? I reiterate that this view must never be allowed to prevail. Once we are in harmony with the spontaneous power of the Vow, we naturally come to realize our indebtedness to Amida Buddha and feel gratitude toward our teachers."

VII

"The nenbutsu is the one unobstructed path. This is because the gods of heaven and earth bow down in reverence before the devotee of the true faith, but he can never be hindered by the realm of demons or by adherents to heterodox views. No evil deed can bring upon him the retribution of karma, nor can any good deed that he might do surpass the nenbutsu. Hence I call this the one unobstructed path."

VIII

"For the devotee the calling of the nenbutsu is neither religious observance nor moral worthiness. It is not a religious observance because it is not done by his own design. It is not a moral deed since it is none of his own doing. As it springs wholly from the other-power and surpasses all self-effort, I say that for the devotee the calling of the nenbutsu is neither religious observance nor moral worthiness."

IX

"Even when I call the nenbutsu, I rarely feel like dancing for joy, nor do I have   729c
any fervent longing to be reborn in the Pure Land. Why is this so?" I asked.

"There was once a time when I, Shinran, also had doubts on this question.
Now, Yuienbō, I find you sharing the same doubts. But when I reflect on this
more deeply, I realize that our rebirth in the Pure Land is all the more assured
because we cannot feel like dancing for joy as we would wish. That is how
you should think of this problem. It is defilement by evil passions that
oppresses our hearts and prevents us from rejoicing. But since Amida Buddha,
knowing this already, has called us 'common beings defiled by ignorance,'
I realize that the compassionate vow of the other-power was made for the
benefit of just such defiled beings as ourselves, and so I feel it all the more
worthy of trust.

"Moreover, when we have no longing to be reborn instantly in the Pure
Land, if we fall even slightly ill, we feel helpless with the fear of death. This
is likewise because of our evil passions. How strong indeed must they be when
we find it so hard to leave our native land of suffering, where we have been
wandering through birth and death for numberless *kalpa*s, and when we can
feel no longing for Amida's Pure Land, where we have yet to be reborn! We
are reborn into that land when we have exhausted, even though reluctantly,
our karmic relations to this world of suffering and end our lives helplessly. So
Amida pities above all those who feel no urgent longing to go to the Pure Land.
Reflecting on this, we realize all the more how trustworthy is Amida's great
compassionate vow and how firmly our rebirth is assured. If, on the contrary,   730a
our hearts were to rejoice with an eager aspiration for rebirth in the Pure Land,
we might believe that we had no evil passions at all."

X

"The meaning of the nenbutsu lies in its freedom from contrivance, because
it is imponderable, indescribable, and inconceivable," the Master said.

Separate Foreword

Now years ago, when the Master was still alive, those sharing the one faith
and aspiring to the Land of Reward to come, who with a common aim under-

13

went the hardships of travelling to Kyoto the distant capital, all had the privilege of hearing the teachings from him at the same time. And yet it is rumored of late that among the numberless converts, both young and old, who recite the nenbutsu under the guidance of those direct disciples, there are not a few who expound doctrines contrary to the Master's intention. The following are some of those groundless doctrines.

XI

On meeting with illiterate callers of the nenbutsu, such persons dismay them by asking: "Do you utter the nenbutsu with faith in the wonder of the Original Vow or with faith in the wonder of the Name?" but without clearly distinguishing between the two. This distinction should be looked into carefully.

730b

Since through the wonder of his Original Vow Amida realized the Name, which is easy to hold in mind and to call, and promised that he would receive those who did so, we utter the nenbutsu in the faith that through the working of Amida's will we shall be delivered from the cycle of birth and death by the wonder of Amida's great compassionate vow. Understanding it in this way, we shall be perfectly in accord with his Original Vow and shall be reborn into the true Land of Reward with no room for self-will at all. In this sense, if we have faith in the wonder of the Vow, it embodies the wonder of the Name, and so the wonder of the Vow and the wonder of the Name are one and not two. Again, if some think that good deeds are a help and bad deeds a hindrance to rebirth, then by this distinction they are not trusting in the wonder of the Vow, but are calling the nenbutsu by their own efforts. Such followers lack real faith in the wonder of the Name. And yet, even though wanting in faith, they may still be reborn in the borderland of the Western Paradise (also called the realm of sloth and pride, the castle of doubt, or the matrix palace) and will at last attain rebirth in the Land of Reward by virtue of the vow of ultimate deliverance. All this is accomplished by the wonder of the Name, which is no different from the wonder of the Vow, for they are one.

XII

Some hold the view that those who do not read or study the sutras and commentaries will not be assured of attaining rebirth in the Pure Land. This view is not worth taking seriously. Various scriptures that make clear the truth of

14

the other-power stress that we are certain to attain buddhahood only when we have faith in the Original Vow and recall the Name. So for rebirth in the Pure Land what else do we need to study?

To be sure, those who are uncertain of this truth ought to study hard if they wish to grasp the purport of the Original Vow. But how pitiful indeed if, after all their reading and study of the sutras and commentaries, they still fail to grasp the real meaning! Because the Name can easily be repeated by those who are unlettered and ignorant of what the sutras and commentaries mean, it is called the easy path; whereas the path of sages, being founded upon learning, is called the difficult path. There is, moreover, a passage in Shinran Shōnin's letters testifying to this problem:

730c

> I am doubtful of the immediate rebirth in the Pure Land of anyone who engages in scholarly pursuits while mistakenly attached to thoughts of wealth and fame.

At present, followers of the exclusive practice of the Name and adherents of the path of sages are engaged in disputes about doctrine, each holding that his own is superior and that of his opponent inferior. Thus adversaries of the teaching arise and calumny against the Dharma is committed. Does not this amount to reviling one's own teaching?

Supposing that followers of other schools ridicule us by saying that the Name is meant for those of low intelligence and that this teaching is shallow and inferior, we should avoid any dispute and reply: "As we are convinced that the ignorant who are poorly gifted and illiterate like ourselves will be delivered by faith, for us this is the supreme doctrine, even though it may seem contemptible to those of higher ability. Although other teachings may be superior, we cannot practice them because they are beyond our powers. Since the original intention of all the buddhas is to free everyone from birth and death, we request those of other views not to interfere with us." If we treat them without malice, who then will harm us?

Besides, "Where there are disputes, all kinds of evil passions are aroused." The wise person should stay as far away as possible from controversy, as this passage in the *Scripture of the Accumulation of Jewels* testifies.

The late Master said:

731a As the Buddha foretold, some would trust in this teaching, while others would revile it. Since I already have faith in it, whereas others find fault with it, I know that what the Buddha said is true. Because of this, we should feel confident that our rebirth is all the more certain. If, by chance, no one happened to speak ill of the teaching, we might wonder why, when there are those with faith, there are no fault-finders. I do not wish to say that the doctrine must necessarily be reviled, but simply that the Buddha, foreseeing that there would be scoffers as well as faithful, warned his followers not to harbor doubts.

Nowadays some appear to study only in preparation to engage in disputes and controversies and to counter the calumny of others. But the more one studies the more one should realize the true intention of the Buddha and become aware of the infinitude of his compassionate vow as well. Only he is worthy of the name of scholar who explains to those in doubt that, as poorly gifted people, they can attain rebirth, and that the Original Vow makes no distinction between good and evil, pure and impure. Anyone who asserts that study is necessary, intimidating even those in whom the Name is called selflessly in accord with the Vow, is a diabolical obstruction to the Dharma and an adversary of the Buddha. Not only does such a person lack faith in the other-power, but he

731b is also sure to lead others into error. We should be particularly cautious about acting against the intentions of our late Master. At the same time such opponents are to be pitied for not being in accord with Amida's Original Vow.

XIII

It is said that those who are unafraid of evil because of Amida's Original Vow presume too much on its miraculous power, and so fail to attain rebirth. Those who speak thus betray their doubt of the Original Vow and their ignorance of good and evil deeds in past and present lives. The arising of good thoughts is caused by past good, while evil thoughts arise because of the working of past evil.

The late Master said:

Even a defilement as minute as a speck of dust on the tip of one hair of rabbit's fur or sheep's wool could not come about without karmic causes in the past.

On another occasion the Master asked me: "Yuienbō, do you have complete trust in whatever I say to you?"

"Yes, I have," I answered.

"If so, will you obey me in whatever I ask you to do?"

To this I respectfully gave my assent.

"For example," the Master continued, "Will you kill one thousand people? If so, you will be assured of rebirth."

"With all due respect to your words," I replied, "I do not feel capable at present of killing even one person."

"If so," Shinran asked, "Why did you just now promise that you would not disobey me?" and then continued: "From this you should learn that, if you could do anything you wished, then should you be told to kill a thousand people so as to attain rebirth, you could commit murder. But since there is no karmic cause within you to murder even one person, you simply cannot kill; it is not because you have good intentions. Even though you had no intention to kill others, it could come about that you might murder a hundred or even a thousand people. This teaches us that, because we falsely assume that we gain rebirth when our intentions are good but do not when they are bad, we fail to realize that we are delivered solely by the miraculous power of the Original Vow." 731c

There was once a man who had become attached to a false idea. He taught that because of the all-embracing vow to deliver evildoers, one should deliberately commit evil deeds as a means of attaining rebirth. When news of his various misdemeanors reached the ears of Shinran Shōnin, he admonished his followers in a letter with these words: "Just because you possess the antidote, do not become addicted to the poison." With this saying he meant to put an end to such perverse attachments; he did not at all mean that evil deeds could obstruct rebirth.

"If we could trust in the Original Vow only by observing the moral precepts and by obeying the many rules of the Order," he said, "how could we ever deliver ourselves from birth and death? Faithless as we are, it is only when we encounter the Original Vow that we can wholly rely upon it. Nonetheless, we can never commit evil unless it is karmically caused."

Again the Master said:

This holds true for those who gain their livelihood by casting nets in the sea or fishing by the river, those who hunt birds and beasts in the mountains and fields, and those who trade or till the soil.

732a   Shinran Shōnin remarked that "When karmic conditions are opportune, we are capable of committing any evil!" and yet at present there are some who assume a pious air of seeking the afterlife, as though only good people were entitled to call the Name; and they post up notices in halls of worship prohibiting admission to those who have transgressed. Are not such people only pretending outwardly to be wise and zealous, while inwardly remaining false and deceitful?

Even those evil deeds committed because of overconfidence in the Vow are caused by past karma. That being so, if we leave all deeds, good and bad alike, to karma and place our sole reliance on the Original Vow, we are really in conformity with the other-power. Bear in mind that the *Tract on Faith Alone* warns us: "How can we consider ourselves too debased to be reclaimed, when we cannot measure the magnitude of Amida's power?"

Our faith in the other-power is confirmed all the more because our hearts feel overconfident in their reliance on the Original Vow. It might possibly be better for us if we could have faith in the Original Vow after we have rid ourselves of evil karma and defilements, because then we would not need to have any overreliance on it. But if we were able to rid ourselves of all defilements, we would already be buddhas, for whom the Vow fulfilled by five *kalpa*s of contemplation would not be needed. Those who admonish others not to be overreliant on the Original Vow nonetheless themselves appear to be filled with defilements and impurities. Are they not also placing too much reliance on the Vow? Just what kinds of evil are meant by "having too much reliance on the Vow" and "not having too much reliance on it"? After all, is not this a shallow argument?

XIV

732b   There are some who insist that one should believe that the heavy burden of evil karma accumulated during eight thousand million *kalpa*s is wiped out by a single calling of the Name.

This assertion seems to refer to one who has committed the ten evils or the five grave offenses, and has never called the Name during his lifetime but who, when faced with death, for the first time meets with a good teacher of the Way. This teacher then instructs him that with one calling of the Name the evils of eight thousand million *kalpa*s will be wiped out, and that with ten callings of the Name the grave karmic burden of ten times eight thousand million *kalpa*s will be expunged, and so rebirth attained. This passage in the *Contemplation Sutra* concerning one calling and ten callings was perhaps referred to in order to make us realize the gravity of the ten evils and the five grave offenses. It points out the benefit of the extinction of evils, but it still falls short of our faith. This is because at the instant when the single thought of faith arises in the heart by Amida's light shining on it, one is endowed with the diamond[like] faith, and the rightly established state has already been reached. When one's lifetime is over, all defilements and hindrances are transformed into the realization that there is no birth and no death.

How can such debased evildoers as we are be delivered from birth and death without his compassionate vow? Bear this thought in mind and regard all the callings of the nenbutsu throughout your life solely as an expression of your indebtedness to Amida's great compassionate heart and of your gratitude for his favor.

Those who are convinced that each calling of the Name can erase the effects of their evil karma are really trying to wipe them out so as to attain rebirth by their own efforts. If this were true, since every thought that we have during our lives binds us to birth and death, rebirth would only be possible by calling the Name without cease up to the very moment of death. But meanwhile, because the effects of past karma have their own limit, we might die without right mindfulness through meeting with an unexpected accident or through being afflicted by the agony of disease, and in the event the Name would be difficult to call. How then could we wipe out the effects of evil committed during that interval? Do such people [of evil karma] insist that, unless the effects of evil karma be effaced, our rebirth is unattainable?

Even though, because of unforeseen events, we may do wrong and die without calling the Name, if we place our trust in the vow that embraces all and forsakes none, we shall immediately gain rebirth. Moreover, even if we

732c

19

are able to call the Name during our last moments, we shall still only be expressing our gratitude to Amida, placing our reliance all the more on him as the moment of our enlightenment draws nearer. The desire to wipe out the effects of past offenses is still self-power, and this is the intention of one who prays to maintain equanimity during his last moments. This shows that he lacks the faith of the other-power.

XV

in previous life

There are those who claim that we have already gained enlightenment, even while our bodies are still defiled by the passions. This view is quite unacceptable to us. To attain buddhahood while still in this body is the essence of the secret teachings of Shingon [school] and is the result of the three esoteric practices. The purification of the six senses is taught by the One Vehicle of the *Lotus Sutra,* and this is attained by practicing the four peaceful observances. But these are all stages along the difficult path, which can be followed only by those specially endowed and belong to the enlightenment attainable only by meditational methods. The basic principle of the other-power teachings of the Pure Land school is to gain enlightenment in the next life, since it follows the path of the assurance of faith. Besides, it is the easy path that can be followed by those of poor ability and is a teaching that does not discriminate between good and evil adherents.

Because, moreover, it is almost impossible to eliminate defilements and hindrances during this lifetime, even the holy monks who practice Shingon and Tendai methods still look forward to reaching enlightenment in the next life. How much truer is this of those of us who lack discipline and wisdom! Yet even we can cross over the painful ocean of birth and death on board the ship of Amida's Vow. As soon as we have reached the shore of the Pure Land, the dark clouds of the defilements will instantly be cleared away and the enlightening moon of buddhahood will at once appear. We can only claim 733a to be enlightened when we are at one with the light that shines unobstructed in the ten directions to benefit all sentient beings.

Do those who claim that they have already attained enlightenment while in their earthly bodies freely expound the Dharma to benefit all beings by manifesting in various bodily transformations possessing the thirty-two major

20

and eighty minor marks of physical perfection, as Śākyamuni did? For these form the paradigm of enlightenment attained in this life.

A hymn in Japanese says:

> In that instant when faith as hard as diamond is established, the light of Amida's heart enfolds us in its protection and we are forever separated from birth and death.

The meaning of this hymn is that, because at the moment when faith is established we are embraced once and for all and never after forsaken, we shall never again wander through the six realms of existence. This is why we are said to be "separated forever from birth and death." Why should this be misunderstood as "attaining enlightenment"? How regrettable! Shinran Shōnin said: "I learned from my master that in the Pure Land teaching one has faith in the Original Vow during this life and that one attains enlightenment in the Pure Land."

XVI

Some insist that the devotee of the nenbutsu should repent whenever he chances to lose his temper, to do wrong, or to quarrel with his fellows. This view savors of eliminating evil and practicing good.

For the devotee of singleminded and exclusive practice of the nenbutsu this change of heart happens only once, when he who has hitherto been ignorant of the true teachings of the other-power of the Original Vow now realizes through Amida's wisdom that he will not attain rebirth in the Pure Land with his habitual moral outlook, and so abandons his former views and henceforth relies solely upon the Original Vow. This is the true meaning of conversion.

733b

If it were necessary to repent all errors, morning and evening, in order to gain rebirth, the vow that embraces all and forsakes none would have been made in vain, since before a person could repent and dwell in tender forbearance, his life might first end between one breath and the next.

Such people give lip service to the power of the Vow, but in their hearts they still secretly harbor the thought that, although the Vow is said to have been meant for all people, in truth it will only be good people who are saved. It is to be deplored that, by so thinking, those who doubt the effectiveness of the Vow and are wanting in trust in the other-power will be born in the borderland of the Western Paradise.

Once faith has been firmly established, rebirth is gained by the favor of Amida, and therefore not through one's own efforts. The more we rely on the power of the Vow as we realize our evil karma, the more will tender forbearance spontaneously arise in us.

In all that concerns rebirth we should always gratefully bear in mind, without any pretension to wisdom, our deep indebtedness to Amida's favor. The natural outcome is that the nenbutsu is called. Lack of artfulness on our part is called "naturalness," which in truth is the working of the other-power. 733c In spite of this I have heard of those who knowingly say that there is some other kind of "naturalness." How regrettable this is!

XVII

There are others who claim that he who gains rebirth in the borderland of the Western Paradise will ultimately fall into hell. In what scriptural source is this view to be found? It is deplorable that such an assertion should have been made by those with pretensions to scholarship. How do they dare to interpret the sacred scriptures and commentaries?

I heard from my master that devotees who lack faith will be reborn in the borderland of the Western Paradise because of their doubt in the Original Vow, but that when the karma of their doubt is exhausted, they will attain enlightenment in the true Land of Reward. Since devotees of the true faith are few in number, most followers are recommended to seek rebirth in the transformed Pure Land. And so to assert that all their aspirations will ultimately prove to be in vain would amount to accusing the Buddha of having led them astray!

XVIII

Again there are still others who say that, depending on the amount offered to the Buddhist Order, one will become a greater or smaller buddha. How utterly nonsensical this is! Such a view is ludicrous. First, one ought not to try to delimit the size of the Buddha, for when the stature of the supreme teacher of the Pure Land is described in the scriptures, this is an expedient form referring to his spiritual body.

Since Amida embodies the realization of ultimate truth, surpassing all forms, long or short, square or round, and also all colors, blue, yellow, red, white, and black, how then can his stature be determined as large or small?

When it is said in the scriptures that by calling the nenbutsu one will receive a vision of an apparitional buddha, this seems to have given rise to the popular belief that by calling the Name in a loud voice, the devotee will see a large buddha, and in a soft voice, a small one. The misinterpretation mentioned at the beginning must have derived from some such popular belief.   734a Offerings to the Order should be regarded as the practice of the perfection of generosity. But if faith is lacking, no matter what precious offering one may make to the Buddha or to one's master, it will prove to no avail. Yet although one does not offer even a single sheet of paper or the smallest amount of money but in his heart is devoted to the other-power with deep faith, his attitude will be in accord with the true intention of the Original Vow.

In all these deviations from the true faith by those who would intimidate their fellows under the pretense of upholding the Dharma, are they not themselves motivated by worldly greed?

Afterword

Such misinterpretations as these have definitely arisen through deviations of faith. There is a story told by our late Master Shinran that while Hōnen was alive he had many disciples among whom few were of the same faith. A dispute once arose between Shinran (then called Zenshin) and his fellow disciples because he had stated that his faith and that of Hōnen were the same. Such disciples as Seikanbō and Nenbutsubō opposed him in forceful words, saying: "How can your faith, Zenshin, possibly be the same as that of our master Hōnen?"

Shinran's reply was:

> It would be absurd if I were to claim that I was Hōnen's equal in wisdom and learning, for his are vast; but regarding our faith in rebirth, there is no difference at all, for his faith and mine are one and the same. *give by Amida*

As they were still in doubt, there was nothing left but to submit the question to Master Hōnen for his decision. When the matter was explained to him,   734b Hōnen said:

My faith was conferred by the Buddha and so was Zenshin's; therefore they are one. Those who hold a separate faith are the least likely to be reborn in the same Pure Land as I, Genkū.

From this I deduce that even now among followers who seem single-heartedly and exclusively devoted to the nenbutsu, there are some whose faith is not at one with Shinran's.

All I have said is only needless repetition, but still I have written it down so that, whenever I hear the doubts of my fellow devotees, I shall be able to convey to them as long as I continue to live, like a dewdrop on a withered leaf, what I learned from my master; and also because I fear that after my death further confusions may arise. Should followers who put forth such false views attempt to mislead you, you ought to read carefully those scriptures favored and followed by the late Master which were in accord with his deepest convictions.

From our viewpoint, in all the scriptures the true and actual teachings are intermingled with the provisional and expedient. The Master's real intention was that you should discard the provisional and keep to the actual, put aside the expedient and abide by the true. You should take great care not to mis-
734c   understand the scriptures. As a standard of the true faith, I have chosen certain important passages, which I have appended to this book.

The Master used to say:

> When I reflect deeply on the Vow that Amida fulfilled after five *kalpa*s of contemplation, I find that it was for me, Shinran, alone! How compassionate, therefore, is the Original Vow of Amida, who was moved to free me from so many karmic defilements!

Reflecting again on the Master's words, I find them little different from Shandao's golden saying:

> We should realize that in truth we are ordinary unenlightened beings involved in birth and death, who from the remotest past up to the present time have been forever floundering in samsara (birth and death), and that we have no way of freeing ourselves.

And so, by giving himself as an example, the Master's words were meant to awaken us to our twofold ignorance: we are deluded as to the depth of our transgressions and unaware of the breadth of Amida's beneficence. For others as well as myself speak only of good and evil without heeding the beneficence of Amida. As Shinran said:

> I am completely ignorant of good and evil. If I could know what good was as totally as Amida does, then I could claim to know good; and if I knew evil as totally as Amida does, then I could claim to know evil. But I must confess that we are all ordinary beings beset by defiling passions and that everything in our world is as transient as a burning house. All things are illusory and delusive and have no truth in them. The nenbutsu alone is true.   735a

Indeed, I myself as well as others speak only of idle things, of which the most regrettable is that when we discuss among ourselves or explain to others the meaning of faith, some impute to the Master words that he did not utter, merely to silence their opponents and put an end to the discussion. This is most deplorable, and we should be careful to discriminate in this regard.

All these are not my own words and yet they may sound strange, because I am not well versed in the scriptures and commentaries nor have I grasped the depths of the doctrine. But I have remembered and set down here only a hundredth part of what the late Master Shinran taught. What a pity if one fortunate enough to call the Name should not be reborn directly into the Land of Reward but should stop short at its borders!

So that there may be no divergences of faith among followers of our school, I have taken up my brush in tears and have written this down. It should be called the *Tannishō or Passages Deploring Deviations of Faith,* and ought not to be indiscriminately made public.

Appendix

During the reign of retired Emperor Gotoba (1180–1239), Hōnen Shōnin (1133–1212) spread the nenbutsu teaching of the other-power based on Amida's Original Vow. Thereupon the monks of Kōfukuji in Nara petitioned the Imperial Household, indicting Hōnen on charges that some of his disciples committed a misdemeanor.

The following were the accused, who were found guilty on the groundless   735b evidence of hearsay: Hōnen and seven of his disciples were exiled, and four of his disciples suffered capital punishment.

Hōnen Shōnin was sentenced to exile in the county of Hata in Tosa province (present-day Kōchi prefecture) and as a criminal was given the name of "Fujii Motohiko, male, aged seventy-six" and so on. Shinran [Shōnin] was sentenced to exile in Echigo province (present-day Niigata prefecture) under the criminal's name of "Fujii Yoshizane, aged thirty-five." Jōenbō was exiled to Bingo province (present-day Hiroshima prefecture); Chōsai Zenkōbō to Hōki province (present-day Tottori prefecture); Kōkabubō to Izu peninsula (present-day Shizuoka prefecture); and Gyōkū Hōhonbō to Sado Island (part of present-day Niigata prefecture).

Although Kōsai Jōgakubō and Zennebō [Shōkū] were also sentenced to banishment elsewhere, the ex-Daisōjō, Jien (1155–1225) of Mudōji [on Mount Hiei] offered to keep them under his custody.

Thus eight people in all were sentenced to exile. The four who suffered capital punishment were Saii Zenshakubō, Shōganbō, Jūrenbō, and Anrakubō.

These sentences were passed by the Hōin (a high monastic title) Sonchō, who held the second court rank.

Now that Shinran had been defrocked and given a secular name, he was neither a monk nor a layman. He therefore adopted the character Toku ("bald-headed") for his family name, and this was subsequently given official approval. The judicial document is said to be kept even now in the registration office. After his exile, Shinran always signed his name: "Shinran the Bald-headed."

Postscript

This sacred scripture is one of the most valuable texts of our school. Those insufficiently matured in faith should not be allowed indiscriminately to read it.

(signed)
Shaku Rennyo

RENNYO SHŌNIN OFUMI
THE LETTERS OF RENNYO

Contents

Translators' Introduction

Rennyo (1415–1499) was the eighth head priest of the Honganji branch of the Jōdo Shin sect, which recognizes Shinran (1173–1262) as its founder. Within the Honganji, Rennyo is revered as the restorer of Shinran's teaching; under Rennyo's leadership the movement emerged as one of the most widespread and powerful religious movements in medieval Japan. He is best known for his hundreds of pastoral letters, *Ofumi* or *Gobunshō*, written in colloquial Japanese for the instruction of participants in the Shin tradition. Eighty of these letters are given here under the title of *Rennyo Shōnin Ofumi* (*Letters of Rennyo*).

The immediacy of Rennyo's letters derives from the stark uncertainty of the world in which he lived and from the widely accepted view that Japan had entered *mappō*, the last Dharma age, when, according to Shinran's teaching, the only way to be born in the Pure Land was to entrust oneself singleheartedly to the other-power of Amida Buddha. Rennyo's particular contribution to his tradition was to clarify that process of entrusting; this is the focus of many of his letters. In addition, we find within the letters identification and repudiation of heterodox teachings and practices, an interpretation of the nenbutsu patterned on that of Shandao (613–681) (Jp. Zendō), and an emphatic message that salvation is open to all—that "when . . . other-power faith is decisively settled, no distinction at all is made between male and female, old and young" (Letter I:2).

Collections of Rennyo's letters began to appear during the tenure of his son, Jitsunyo (1458–1525), the ninth head priest of the Honganji. The letters were hand-copied, a few at a time, and authorized for circulation under Jitsunyo's official seal. A memoir by another son Jitsugo (1492–1584), attests to the profound reverence accorded them: "The letters are to be regarded as the Tathāgata's teaching. . . . When you hear the words, you are listening directly to Amida" [*Goichidaiki kikigaki*, T.83:818b]. Gradually a plan evolved for a standardized collection: eighty letters, the *Gojō ofumi*, were selected out of the several hundred available. Five additional letters (not translated here) were included, four of which are designated as *Natsu ofumi*, letters of summer; the fifth is the *Gozokushō*,

Shinran's genealogy. The person generally recognized as responsible for the compilation is Jitsunyo's son Ennyo (1491–1521).

It was during the tenure of Shōnyo (1516–1554), the tenth head priest of the Honganji, that the collection took printed form (his seal is affixed to the Taishō edition text); since that time it has been widely distributed within the Shin community. These eighty-five letters are included in the third volume of the *Shinshū shōgyō zensho* (Kyoto: Ōyagi Kōbundō, 1969–70) and also in various editions of the *Shinshū seiten.* The major collection of extant letters is Inaba Masamaru's *Rennyo Shōnin ibun* (Kyoto: Hōzōkan, 1948; reprinted 1983), composed of two hundred and twenty-one letters held to be authentic and, insofar as possible, listed chronologically.

The *Gojō ofumi* is divided into five fascicles, of which the first four are arranged chronologically. Fascicle I contains fifteen letters written between Bunmei 3 (1471), 7.15, and Bunmei 5 (1473), 9.22, from Yoshizaki in the Hokuriku. The fifteen letters in fascicle II are also from Yoshizaki; they were written between Bunmei 5 (1473), 12.8, and Bunmei 6 (1474), 7.9. Fascicle III contains thirteen letters written between Bunmei 6 (1474), 7.14, and Bunmei 8 (1476), 7.18; ten of these were written from Yoshizaki, two from Deguchi. The fifteen letters in Fascicle IV were written between Bunmei 9 (1477), 1.8, and Meiō 7 (1498), 11.21, the year before Rennyo's death. The twenty-two letters in Fascicle V are undated; certain ones, however, are identical to passages in dated letters.

Letter titles do not appear in the Taishō edition; those provided in this translation are translations of titles (based on first lines of the text) found in Junjō Ōe and Shōjitsu Ōhara, eds., *Shinshū seiten (Shinshū Scriptures)* (Kyoto: Nagata Bunshōdō, 1956, 1969, reprint), pp. 660–802. Titles also appear, in slightly different form, in Yūsen Kashiwabara, ed., *Shinshū seiten (Shinshū Scriptures)* (1935) (Kyoto: Hōzōkan, 1969, reprint), pp. 785–865.

What did those responsible for the compilation of the *Gojō ofumi* wish to convey through their selection? Although the letters of the first four fascicles are arranged chronologically, few indicate the passage of time. The reader is barely aware that the eighty letters cover a period of twenty-seven years. They tell very little of Rennyo's activities or of his personal life. At a time when the Honganji was gaining extraordinary power, the intention appears to have been to present those letters that were meaningful apart from particular historical circumstances, that clarified points essential to the tradition, and that established its distinctive marks.

Major issues in the translation of Rennyo's letters into English focus on the terms *shinjin, anjin,* and *tasuke tamae.* How should the first two, concepts of deep significance for the tradition, be translated, and should the third be translated in as direct a manner as it appears to be written?

In sixty-three of the eighty letters, the term *shinjin* occurs a total of two hundred seventy-four times in various contexts, including quotations; the negative *fushinjin* occurs twice. In thirty-two of the letters, the term *anjin* occurs a total of forty-seven times and the negative *mianjin* occurs three times. In addition, the first character *shin* of the compound *shinjin* serves as a noun on ten occasions and the negative *fushin* on five.

Until recently, translators of Shinran's writings, including Daisetz Teitarō Suzuki, have rendered *shinjin* into English as "faith." Translators in the Ryūkoku Translation Center in Kyoto continue to do so, clarifying their choices of these and other terms with rich annotation. Previous translations of Rennyo's letters, recognizing that in many instances the meaning of *anjin* is indistinguishable from that of *shinjin,* have translated both terms as "faith."

On the other hand, we have noted the precedent set by the translators of the Shin Buddhism Translation Series (Kyoto: Honganji International Center, 1978–). In their task of translating the entire corpus of Shinran's works, they have chosen to introduce the term "shinjin" (without italics) into the English text. They argue eloquently that most of the possible connotations of the English word "faith" are entirely inappropriate for their tradition and cannot convey the nuances of *shinjin* without misleading preconceptions. It is possible that Rennyo's core concept *anjin* might be treated similarly and introduced without italics, with the prospect of both terms becoming part of our English vocabulary. The Shin Buddhism Translation Series approach has much to commend it and will continue to contribute an essential perspective to the ongoing translation of the Shin Buddhist sense of the oneness of the human heart and mind and the Buddha's.

Here, however, we have chosen to translate *shinjin* as "faith" and *anjin* as "settled mind" or "faith," depending on context (see, for example, Letter V:13). To clarify which Japanese term, other than *shinjin,* is being translated as "faith," we have inserted the corresponding Japanese term into the text following each occurrence of the nouns *shin, fushin, fushinjin, anjin, mianjin,* or *shingyō* (when they mean "faith" or the lack of it). While the Shin Buddhism Translation Series approach preserves what is unique to Shin Buddhist tradition, we have found that the particular meaning of these terms in the tradition does in fact draw out and underscore the deepest meanings of "faith" and "settled mind" as general religious terms. As Rennyo clearly explains, *shinjin* has two aspects in dynamic interrelationship: one of these is the entrusting mind of sentient beings who turn to Amida to save them; the other is the mind of the Buddha, which is itself the entrusting mind given to sentient beings, bringing them to buddhahood in the afterlife. *Shinjin* is a concept perhaps best translated consistently by the word "faith"—a faith that is salvific truth empowered and given by that which is entirely beyond human effort and calculative thinking. Granted that the term "faith" tends to focus on the mind of the person to be saved, what other English term could at the same time hint at the other pole of the paradox—in this instance, the salvific mind of Amida Buddha?

Anjin, "settled mind," suggests the mind in which "the peace that passes all understanding" is settled once and for all, beyond all shadow of doubt. Since *anjin* is translated literally as "easily [attained] mind" (Letter II:7), it might seem that the resulting "serene mind" or "serenity," rather than the compound "settled mind," would be the choice more closely parallel to "faith." "Serenity," however, fails to suggest the paradox implicit in *anjin,* in that it emphasizes the quality of mind of the person saved at the expense of the underlying decisiveness—the diamondlike quality—of the mind of Amida. This is evident in translating the term *anjin ketsujō:* it seems quite possible to speak of a person in whom "the settled mind is established" (Letter I:3) but somewhat awkward to refer to one in whom "serenity is established." Since it is the fact of definite establishment that leads to serenity, "settled mind," despite the lack of parallelism, may be an acceptable choice.

A final point: of the fifty occurrences of *anjin* and *mianjin* in the text, the term "faith" has been the translation preferable to "settled mind" on at least nineteen occasions. Thus "faith" appears to be able to serve in many instances for both *shinjin* and *anjin*—each of which lends a particular emotional overtone to their shared meaning. "Faith" seems appropriate in this context as well, for it has the capacity to convey a sense of fundamental wholeness suggested by few other English terms.

In considering the issue of *tasuke tamae,* it is apparent from the thrust of Rennyo's writings that the phrase should not be literally interpreted as a request

[Tasuke tamae]

to Amida, "Please save me." The practice of reciting the nenbutsu as a plea for salvation was common among participants in other strands of the Pure Land tradition. Rennyo, in contrast, stated in his earliest extant letter (not included among the eighty) that Honganji followers were not even to think, "Buddha, please save me" in saying the nenbutsu, but to understand it solely as an expression of gratitude. For this reason, we have translated the phrase indirectly, with slight variations according to context. For example, Letter I:7 reads:

> For when there arises the one thought-moment [of faith] in which we entrust ourselves to Amida without any double-mindedness and realize *that* [*Amida*] *saves us.* . . . (italics added)

Letter III:2 reads:

> *Na-mu* means . . . entrusting ourselves without double-mindedness [to Amida] *to save us,* [bringing us to buddhahood] in the afterlife." (italics added)

Our position is that Rennyo adopted a phrase that was familiar to many of those attracted to his leadership of the Honganji Shin sect in the Hokuriku, bringing to it an other-power interpretation that was radically different from the customary understanding of the idea in the Pure Land tradition as a whole.

For over half a millennium, Rennyo's letters have served as holy texts for participants in the Shin sect. In traditional households, reading the letters and hearing them read daily has, along with the recitation of the *Shōshinge,* steadily nurtured and shaped Shin piety. Only the *Tannishō,* a text "rediscovered" in the past century, is of comparable significance in presenting Shinran's core teachings in popular form.

Among the many reference works consulted in the course of translating the *Rennyo Shōnin Ofumi,* two volumes were ever at hand: the first, a line-by-line commentary by the late Shin scholar Shirō Sugi, *Gobunshō kōwa* (Kyoto: Nagata Bunshōdō, 1933; 1979 reprint); the second, an annotated text and commentary by the specialist in Japanese literature Osamu Izumoji, *Ofumi,* Tōyō Bunko, No. 345 (Tokyo: Heibonsha, 1978). In drawing on traditional sectarian studies as well as on modern literary scholarship, our goal has been to present Rennyo's words clearly and accurately and to find the English equivalents most appropriate for a consistent rendering of technical terms. Readers are encouraged to refer to the glossary appended to this translation and also to glossary entries in the translations of Shinran's works in the volumes in the Shin Buddhism Translation Series and in the annotated texts in the Ryūkoku Translation Series (Kyoto: Ryūkoku University, 1962–). Citations in Rennyo's letters from texts found in the *Taishō shinshū daizōkyō* (T.) are so indicated; in several instances, the most likely sources are noted. When Rennyo quotes a passage from an earlier Buddhist source, we give the Taishō reference to that work. In addition, when the quotation also appears in Shinran's writings, we often provide that reference as an aid to investigation into the continuity of their teaching.

To Professor Masatoshi Nagatomi, Professor Michio Tokunaga, Professor Dennis Hirota, Professor John B. Carman, Professor John Ross Carter, Professor Paul S. Groner, and Professor Edwin D. Craun, we express our particular gratitude for their guidance, support, and example over the years at the moments when they were most needed. Any errors that remain are entirely our own.

RENNYO SHŌNIN OFUMI:
THE LETTERS OF RENNYO

Fascicle I

1. On Followers and Disciples

Someone has asked: "In our tradition, are followers necessarily considered 771a disciples of a particular priest, or do we speak of them as disciples of the Tathāgata and of Master [Shinran]? I have no clear understanding of this. Also, there are some who have informal groups of followers in various places and are determined these days to keep this from the priest of the temple [to which they belong]. As people say that this is inappropriate, I am confused about it also. Please instruct me."

Answer: I consider these questions to be of the utmost importance indeed. I shall state briefly what I have heard in our tradition. Please listen.

The late Master said:

> [I], Shinran, do not have even a single disciple. The reason for this is that when I expound the Tathāgata's Dharma to sentient beings in the ten directions, I am only speaking as the Tathāgata's representative. [I] . . . do not propagate any new Dharma at all; I entrust myself to the Tathā-gata's Dharma and simply teach that to others. Besides that, what do I teach that I would speak of having disciples?

Thus we are one another's companions and fellow practitioners. Because of this, the Master spoke respectfully of "companions and fellow practitioners."

Recently, however, even priests of high position, ignorant of what our 771b school teaches about the settled mind, severely rebuke those among their disciples who happen to go to places where faith is discussed and listen to the Dharma; thus, at times, discord arises. Consequently, since the priests themselves do not clearly hear the reality of faith, and since they deal with their disciples in such a manner, faith is not decisively settled either for them or for their disciples, and their lives then pass in vain. It is truly difficult for them to escape blame for harming themselves and others. This is deplorable, deplorable.

41

An old poem says:

> Long ago,
> Joy
> Was wrapped in my sleeves—
> But, tonight,
> It's more than I can contain!

"Long ago, joy was wrapped in my sleeves" means that in the past, we felt certain—without any clear understanding of the sundry practices and the right practices—that we would be born [in the Pure Land] if we just said the nenbutsu. "But, tonight, it's more than I can contain" means that the joy of saying the nenbutsu in grateful return for the Buddha's benevolence is especially great now that, having heard and understood the difference between the right and the sundry [practices], we have become steadfast and single-hearted and have thus undergone a decisive settling of faith. Because of this, we are so overjoyed that we feel like dancing—hence the joy is "more than I can contain."

Respectfully.

Bunmei 3 (1471), 7.15

2. On Becoming a Priest in the Aspiration for Buddhahood

The fundamental principle of Master Shinran in our tradition is not that one should become a priest in the aspiration for buddhahood or that one should renounce family and separate oneself from worldly attachments; it is simply that when, with [the awakening of] the one thought-moment of taking refuge [in Amida], other-power faith is decisively settled, no distinction at all is made between male and female, old and young. The [*Larger*] *Sutra* describes the state of having attained this faith (*shin*) as "immediately attaining birth [in the Pure Land] and dwelling in [a state of] nonretrogression" (*Daimuryō-jukyō*, T.12:272b; *Jōdo monrui jushō*, T.83:646b); [Tanluan] says in a commentary, "With the awakening of the one thought [of entrusting], we enter the company of those [whose birth] is truly settled" (*Jōdo ronchū*, T.40:826b;

771c

42

Kyōgyōshinshō, T.83:597b). This, then, is what is meant by talk of "not [waiting for Amida to] come to meet [us at the moment of death]" and of "completing the cause [of birth] in ordinary life."

In a hymn, [Shinran] says:

Those who aspire to [birth in] Amida's fulfilled land,
Though outward conditions may vary,
Should truly accept the Name [as promised in] the Primal Vow
And, sleeping or waking, never forget it.

"Outward conditions [may vary]" means that no distinction is made between layperson and priest or between male and female. Next, "should truly accept the Name [as promised in] the Primal Vow and, sleeping or waking, never forget it" means that—no matter what the external form [of our lives] may be, and even if our evil karma includes the ten transgressions and the five grave offenses, or if we are among those who slander the Dharma or lack the seed of buddhahood—if we undergo a turning of the mind and repent, and truly realize deep within that Amida Tathāgata's saving Primal Vow is for just such wretched people, if we entrust ourselves without any double-mindedness to the Tathāgata and, without forgetting, sleeping or waking, are always mindful of Amida, then we are said to be people of faith who rely on the Primal Vow and have attained the decisive mind.

Then, beyond this, even if we say the Name [constantly]—walking, standing, sitting, and lying down—we should think of it as an expression of gratitude for Amida Tathāgata's benevolence. Such a person is called a practitioner who has realized true and real faith and whose birth is decisively settled.

On this hot day
My flowing sweat
May truly be my tears
And what I've written with my brush—
How strange it looks.

Respectfully.
Bunmei 3 (1471), 7.18   772a

43

3. On Hunting and Fishing

First, [realizing] the settled mind in our tradition does not mean that we put a stop to our mind's evil or to the rising of delusions and attachments. Simply carry on with your trade or position of service, hunt and fish. For when we realize deeply that Amida Tathāgata's Primal Vow promises to save such worthless beings as ourselves, who are confused morning and evening by evil karma, when we singleheartedly (without any double-mindedness) rely on the compassionate vow of the one Amida Buddha, and when sincere faith is awakened in us by the realization that Amida saves us, then, without fail, we partake of the Tathāgata's saving work.

Beyond this, when there is a question as to with what understanding we should say the nenbutsu, [the answer is that] we are to say the nenbutsu as long as we live, realizing that it is in gratitude, in return for the gracious benevolence that saves us by giving us the power of entrusting, through which our birth is assured. [Those who do] this are to be called practitioners of faith in whom the settled mind of our tradition is established.

Respectfully.
Bunmei 3 (1471), 12.18

4. Some Questions and Answers

[*Question:*] I am told that Master Shinran's tradition speaks of "completing the cause [of birth in the Pure Land] in ordinary life" and does not adhere to "[Amida's] coming to meet [us at the moment of death]." What does this mean? I do not know anything about "completing the cause [of birth] in ordinary life" or about the significance of "not [waiting for Amida to] come to meet [us at the moment of death]." I would like to hear about this in detail.

772b   *Answer:* Indeed, I consider these questions to be of the utmost importance for our tradition. From the beginning, this school has taught that "with the awakening of the one thought-moment [of faith], the cause [of birth] is completed in ordinary life." After we have understood that it is through the unfolding of past good that we hear and realize in [the midst of] ordinary life that

Amida Tathāgata's Primal Vow saves us, we understand that it is not by our own power but through the gift of other-power, the wisdom of the Buddha, that we become aware of how Amida's Primal Vow came to be. This is the meaning of "completing the cause [of birth] in ordinary life." Thus "completing the cause [of birth] in ordinary life" is a state of mind in which we have heard and fully understood this principle and are convinced that birth is assured; we refer to it as "with the awakening of the one thought-moment, joining the company of those [whose birth is] truly settled," "completing the cause [of birth] in ordinary life," and "immediately attaining birth [in the Pure Land] and dwelling in [a state of] nonretrogression."

Question: I fully understand the concept of "birth [in the Pure Land] with the awakening of the one thought-moment." However, I still do not understand the meaning of "not [waiting for Amida to] come and meet [us at the moment of death]." Would you kindly explain this?

Answer: As for the matter of "not [waiting for Amida to] come to meet [us at the moment of death]," when we realize that "with the awakening of the one thought-moment, we join the company of those [whose birth is] truly settled," there is no longer any need to expect [Amida's] coming. The reason is that "waiting for [Amida to] come to meet [us]" is a matter of concern to those who perform various other practices. For practitioners of true and real faith, it is understood that there is no longer a wait for [Amida's] coming to meet [us] when we immediately receive, with the awakening of the one thought-moment, the benefit of [being protected by] the light that embraces and never abandons.

Therefore, according to the teaching of the Master, "[Amida's] coming to meet [us at the moment of death]" pertains to birth through various other practices; practitioners of true and real faith are embraced and never abandoned, and for this reason, they join the company of those [whose birth is] truly settled. Because they join those who are truly settled, they will attain 772c nirvana without fail. Hence there is no waiting for the moment of death and no reliance on [Amida's] coming to meet [us at that time]. We should bear these words in mind.

Question: Should we understand [the state of] being truly settled and [that of] nirvana as one benefit, or as two?

Answer: The dimension of "the awakening of the one thought-moment" is that of "[joining] the company of those truly settled." This is the benefit [we gain] in the defiled world. Next, it should be understood that nirvana is the benefit to be gained in the Pure Land. Hence we should think of them as two benefits.

Question: Knowing that birth is assured when we have understood as you have explained, how should we understand being told that we must go to the trouble of acquiring faith? I would like to hear about this, too.

Answer: This inquiry is indeed of great importance. That is, the very understanding that conforms to what has been explained above is precisely what we mean by decisively settled faith.

Question: I clearly understand that the state in which faith is decisively settled is described as "completing the cause [of birth] in ordinary life," "not [waiting for Amida to] come to meet [us at the moment of death]," and "[joining] the company of those who are truly settled." However, I do not yet understand whether, after faith is decisively settled, we should say the nenbutsu for the sake of birth in the Land of Utmost Bliss or in gratitude for [Amida] Buddha's benevolence.

773a

Answer: I consider this question, too, to be of great importance. The point is that we must not think of the nenbutsu said after the awakening of the one thought-moment of faith as an act for the sake of birth; it should be understood to be solely in gratitude for the Buddha's benevolence. Therefore, Master Shandao explained it as "spending one's entire life at the upper limit, one thought-moment [of faith] at the lower." It is understood that "one thought-moment at the lower" refers to the settling of faith, and "spending one's entire life at the upper limit" refers to the nenbutsu said in gratitude, in return for the Buddha's benevolence. These are things that should be very thoroughly understood.

Respectfully.
Bunmei 4 (1472), 11.27

5. On Pilgrimage in the Snow

From [the beginning of] this year, an unexpectedly large number of priests and laypeople—men and women from the three provinces of Kashū, Noto, and Etchū—have flocked in pilgrimage to this mountain at Yoshizaki; I am uneasy as to what the understanding of each of these people may be.

The reason for this, first of all, is that in our tradition, assurance of birth in the Land of Utmost Bliss with this life is grounded in our having attained other-power faith. However, within this school, there is no one who has attained firm faith. How can people like this be readily born in the fulfilled land? This matter is of the greatest importance. In what frame of mind have they come here through this snow—having fortunately managed to endure the long journey of five to ten *ri?* I am thoroughly apprehensive about this. But whatever their thinking may have been in the past, I will state in detail what should be   773b borne in mind from now on. Be attentive; listen very carefully.

The point is to keep the matter of other-power faith firmly in mind. Beyond that, you should just say the nenbutsu—walking, standing, sitting, and lying down—in gratitude for [Amida] Buddha's benevolence. With this understanding, the birth that is to come [in the Pure Land] is assured. In the fullness of this joy, go to the temples of the priests who are your teachers, and offer some tangible expression of your gratitude. [One who does] this is to be declared a person of faith who has fully understood the principles of our tradition.

Respectfully.
Bunmei 5 (1473), 2.8

6. On Drowsiness

I don't know why, but recently (this summer), I have been particularly subject to drowsiness, and when I consider why I should be [so] lethargic, I feel without a doubt that the moment of death leading to birth [in the Pure Land] may be close at hand. This thought makes me sad, and I feel in particular the sorrow of parting. And yet, to this very day I have prepared myself with no lack of care, thinking that the time of birth might be imminent. All I continually long for in regard to this, day and night, is that, after [my death], there will be no regression in those among the visitors to this temple whose faith is decisively settled. As things now stand, there should be no difficulties if I die, but each of you is particularly lax in your thinking in regard to birth. As long as you live, you should be as I have described. I am altogether dissatisfied   773c with what each of you has understood. In this life, even tomorrow is uncertain, and no matter what we say, nothing is to any avail when life ends. If our doubts are not clearly dispelled during this life, we will surely [be filled with] regret. I hope that you will bear this in mind.

Respectfully.

This is entrusted to those [assembled] on the other side of the sliding doors. In the years to come, please take it out and read it.

Written on the twenty-fifth day
of the fourth month, Bunmei 5 (1473).

7. A Discussion about Yoshizaki

This past year (fourth year of Bunmei), about the middle of the third month as I recall, a few women of some distinction, accompanied by male attendants, were talking about this mountain. "A temple has recently been built on the summit at Yoshizaki," they said. "What a remarkably interesting place that is! Everyone knows that followers of the sect—priests and laypeople, men and women—flock to the mountain in pilgrimage, particularly from the seven provinces of Kaga, Etchū, Noto, Echigo, Shinano, Dewa, and Ōshū. This is extraordinary for the last [Dharma] age, and does not appear to be insignificant. But we would like to hear in detail how the nenbutsu teaching is presented to each of these followers and, above all, what it means when people say that 'faith' is taught as the most important thing. We, too—because we suffer the bodily existence of women wretched with the burden of deep and heavy evil karma—wish to aspire for birth by hearing and understanding this 'faith.'"

774a

When this inquiry was made of the man [living] on the mountain, he responded, "Without doing anything in particular, but simply realizing that you are wretched beings burdened with the ten transgressions, the five grave offenses, the five obstacles, and the three submissions, you must deeply understand that Amida Tathāgata is the form for saving such persons. For when there arises the one thought-moment [of faith] in which we entrust ourselves to Amida without any double-mindedness and realize that [Amida] saves us, the Tathāgata sends forth eighty-four thousand rays of light with which he graciously embraces us. This is what is meant by saying that 'Amida

48

Tathāgata embraces practitioners of the nenbutsu.' 'Embraces and never abandons' means 'receives and does not discard.' We say that [one whose understanding is in accord with] this is a person who has realized faith. Then, beyond this, we must bear in mind that the nenbutsu, *namu-amida-butsu,* which we say sleeping or waking, standing or sitting down, is that nenbutsu, *namu-amida-butsu,* said by those saved by Amida as an expression of gratitude for Amida's gracious benevolence."

When he had carefully related this, the women and others [who were with them] replied, "There is indeed no way to express our shame over not having   774b entrusted ourselves until now to Amida Tathāgata's Primal Vow, which is so suited to our innate capacities. From now on, we shall steadfastly entrust ourselves to Amida, and, believing singleheartedly that our birth has been accomplished by the saving work of the Tathāgata, we shall bear in mind that the nenbutsu is, after this, a saying of the Name in gratitude for the Buddha's benevolence. There is no way at all to express our thankfulness and awe at having been given this opportunity through inconceivable conditions from the past, and at having heard the incomparable Dharma. Now it is time to say farewell."

And with this, their eyes brimming with tears, they took their leave.

Respectfully.
Bunmei 5 (1473), 8.12

8. On Building at Yoshizaki

Around the beginning of the fourth month of the third year of Bunmei, I just slipped away, without any settled plan, from a place near the Miidera's southern branch temple at Ōtsu, in the Shiga district of Ōmi province, and traveled through various parts of Echizen and Kaga. Then, as this site—Yoshizaki, in the Hosorogi district of [Echizen] province—was particularly appealing, we made a clearing on the mountain, which for many years had been the habitat of wild beasts. Beginning on the twenty-seventh day of the seventh month, we put up a building that might be called a temple. With the passage of time from yesterday to today and so on, three years have elapsed with the seasonal changes.

774c

In the meantime, priests and laypeople, men and women, have flocked here; but as this appears to have no purpose at all, I have prohibited their coming and going as of this year. For, to my mind, the fundamental reason for being in this place is that, having received life in the human realm and having already met with the buddha-dharma, which is difficult to meet, it is indeed shameful if one falls in vain into hell. Thus I have reached a judgment that people who are unconcerned about the decisive settling of nenbutsu faith and attainment of birth in the Land of Utmost Bliss should not gather at this place. This is solely because what is fundamental for us is not reputation and personal gain but simply a concern for enlightenment (*bodhi*) in the afterlife. Therefore let there be no misinterpretation by those who see this or hear about it.

Respectfully.
Bunmei 5 (1473), 9

9. On Avoiding Certain Things

For a long time, people have said uniformly that ours is a ridiculous, degenerate sect. This does indeed point to a certain truth: among those in our tradition, [there are] some who unhesitatingly proclaim our teaching in the presence of those of other schools and other sects. This is a great mistake. Observing our tradition's rules of conduct means keeping firmly to ourselves the teaching transmitted in our tradition and not giving any outward sign of it; those who do this are said to be people of discretion. These days, however, some talk carelessly and without reserve about matters concerning our sect in the presence of those of other schools and other sects; as a result, our tradition is considered

775a

shallow. Because there are some with mistaken views, others think that our sect is degraded and detestable. We should bear in mind that this is not at all the fault of others, but that it is the fault of our own people.

Next, as for the matter of avoiding things that are impure and inauspicious, it is established that in our tradition, within the buddha-dharma, we do not regard any particular thing as taboo. But are there not things that we should avoid in regard to other sects and the civil authorities? Of course, in the presence of those of other sects and other schools, there are certainly things to be avoided. Further, we should not criticize others for avoiding things.

Despite all this, it is clearly seen in many passages of various sutras that those who follow the practice of the buddha-dharma—not only people of the nenbutsu—should not be concerned to such an extent with the avoidance of things. First, a passage in the *Nirvana Sutra* says, "Within the Tathāgata's Dharma, there is no choosing of auspicious days and favorable times" (*Daihatsu nehangyō,* T.12:482b). Also, a passage in the *Sutra of the Samādhi of All Buddhas' Presence* states (*Hanju zanmaikyō,* T.13:901b):

> Laywomen who hear of this *samādhi* and want to practice it . . . take refuge in the Buddha; take refuge in the Dharma; take refuge in the Sangha. Do not follow other paths; do not worship heavenly beings; do not enshrine spirits; do not look for auspicious days.

Although there are other passages similar to these in the sutras, I offer these selections. They teach, in particular, that nenbutsu practitioners should not follow such ways. Let this be thoroughly understood.   775b

Respectfully.
Bunmei 5 (1473), 9

10. On the Wives of the Priests
in Charge of Lodgings
at Yoshizaki

Those who become wives of the priests in charge of lodgings on this mountain at Yoshizaki should be aware that this happens because past conditions in their previous lives are not shallow. This awareness, however, will come about after they have realized that the afterlife is the matter of greatest importance and undergone a decisive settling of faith. Therefore those who are to be wives [of the priests] should, by all means, firmly attain faith.

First of all, because what is known as settled mind in our tradition differs greatly from and is superior to [the understanding of] the Jōdo schools in general, it is said to be the great faith of other-power. Therefore, we should realize that those who have attained this faith—ten out of ten, one hundred out of one hundred—are assured of the birth that is to come [in the Pure Land].

[*Question:*] How should we understand this faith (*anjin*)? We do not know about it in any detail.

51

Answer: This question is indeed of the utmost importance. This is how to attain the faith of our tradition:

To begin with, being women—hence wretched creatures of deep evil karma, burdened with the five obstacles and the three submissions—you were abandoned long ago by the tathāgatas of the ten directions and also by all the buddhas of the three periods; yet Amida Tathāgata alone graciously vowed to save just such persons [as you] and long ago made the Forty-eight Vows. Among these vows, beyond [promising] in the Eighteenth Vow to save all evildoers and women, Amida then made a further vow, the Thirty-fifth, to save women because of the depth of their evil karma and doubts. You should have a deep sense of gratitude for Amida Tathāgata's benevolence in having undergone such painstaking endeavors.

775c

Question: After we have come to realize our thankfulness that Amida Tathāgata made vows time and again in this way to save people like us, then in what frame of mind should we entrust ourselves to Amida? We need to have this explained in detail.

Answer: If you wish to attain faith and entrust yourselves to Amida, first realize that human life endures only as long as a dream or an illusion and that the afterlife [in the Pure Land] is indeed the blissful result in eternity, that human life means the enjoyment of [only] fifty to a hundred years, and that the afterlife is the matter of greatest importance. Abandoning your inclination toward all sundry practices and discarding your tendency to avoid certain things, entrust yourselves singleheartedly and steadfastly to Amida and, without concerning yourselves with other buddhas, bodhisattvas, and the various *kami,* take refuge exclusively in Amida, with the assurance that this coming birth is a certainty. Then, in an outpouring of thankfulness, you should say the nenbutsu and respond in gratitude to Amida Tathāgata's benevolence in saving you. This is the frame of mind of resident priests' wives who have attained faith.

776a

Respectfully.

Bunmei 5 (1473), 9.11

11. On Lightning and Morning Dew

On deep contemplation, we realize that the pleasures of human life last only as long as a flash of lightning or the morning dew, a dream or an illusion. Even if we enjoy a life of pomp and glory and can do as we wish, this is only a matter of some fifty to a hundred years. If the wind of impermanence were to come even now and summon us, would we not suffer illness of one kind or another and die? And indeed, at the time of death, no part of either the family or the wealth on which we have depended for so long can accompany us. Thus, all alone, we must cross the great river of three currents, at the end of the mountain path that we take after death. Let us realize, then, that what we should earnestly aspire to is [birth in the Pure Land in] the afterlife, that the one we should rely upon is Amida Tathāgata, and that the place to which we go after faith is decisively settled is the Pure Land of Serene Sustenance. These days, however, the priests in this region who are nenbutsu people are seriously at variance with the buddha-dharma. That is, they call followers from whom they receive donations "good disciples" and speak of them as "people of faith." This is a serious error. Also, the disciples think that if they just bring an abundance of things to the priests, they will be saved by the priests' power, even if their own power is insufficient. This, too, is an error. And so between the priests and their followers, there is not a modicum of understanding of our tradition's faith. This is indeed deplorable. Without a doubt, neither priests nor disciples will be born in the Land of Utmost Bliss; they will fall in vain into hell.

776b

Even though we lament this, we cannot lament deeply enough; though we grieve, we should grieve more deeply. From now on, therefore, [the priests] should seek out those who fully know the details of the great faith of other-power, let their faith be decisively settled, and then teach the essentials of that faith to their disciples; together, they will surely attain the birth that is to come [in the Pure Land], which is the most important matter.

Respectfully.
Bunmei 5 (1473),
the middle of the ninth month

12. The Chōshōji's Past

For years, the followers at the Chōshōji have been seriously at variance with the buddha-dharma. My reason for saying this, first of all, has to do with the leader of the assembly. He thinks that to occupy the place of honor and drink before everyone else and to court the admiration of those seated around him, as well as that of others, is really the most important aspect of the buddha-dharma. This is certainly of no use for birth in the Land of Utmost Bliss; it appears to be just for worldly reputation.

Now, what is the purpose of monthly meetings in our sect?

Laypeople, lacking wisdom, spend their days and nights in vain; their lives pass by meaninglessly, and, in the end, they fall into the three evil paths. The meetings are occasions when, even if only once a month, just those who practice the nenbutsu should at least gather in the meeting place and discuss their own faith and the faith of others. Recently, however, because matters of faith are never discussed in terms of right and wrong, the situation is deplorable beyond words.

776c

In conclusion, there must definitely be discussions of faith from now on among those at the meetings. For this is how we are to attain birth in the true and real Land of Utmost Bliss.

Respectfully.
Bunmei 5 (1473),
end of the ninth month

13. On the False "Ten *Kalpas*" Teachings in This Region

Recently, some of the nenbutsu people in this region have been using strange terms, insisting that they express the attainment of faith; furthermore, they hold to this as if they knew all about our tradition's faith. In their words, "Faith is not forgetting the benevolence of Amida, who settled our birth [in the Pure Land] from the time of his perfect enlightenment ten *kalpas* ago!" This is a serious error. For even if they know all about Amida Tathāgata's perfect enlightenment, this is useless without knowing the significance of other-power faith, by which we are to attain birth.

Therefore, from now on, they should first of all know the true and real faith of our tradition very thoroughly. That faith is expounded in the *Larger Sutra* as "the threefold entrusting"; in the *Contemplation Sutra,* it is called "the three minds"; and in the *Amida Sutra,* it is expressed as "one mind." Although the terms differ in all three sutras, they are simply meant to express the one mind given to us by other-power. 777a

What, then, do we mean by "faith"?

First of all, when we set aside all sundry practices and steadfastly rely on Amida Tathāgata and, giving no thought to any of the *kami* or to other buddhas, take refuge with singleness of heart exclusively in Amida, the Tathā- gata embraces [us] with his light and never abandons us. This is precisely how the one thought-moment of faith is decisively settled.

After we have understood this, we must bear in mind that the nenbutsu expresses our gratitude to Amida Tathāgata for his benevolence in granting us other-power faith. With this, we are to be declared nenbutsu practitioners in whom faith is decisively settled.

Respectfully.
Written in Bunmei 5 (1473),
in the last part of the ninth month

14. An Admonition
against Slander

Now, among nenbutsu people in our tradition, there must be no slander of other teachings. First of all, in Etchū and Kaga, this applies to Tateyama, Shirayama, and the other mountain temples; in Echizen, to the Heisenji, the Toyoharaji, and others. Indeed, we were specifically cautioned about this long ago in the [*Larger*] *Sutra:* "Excluded [from the Eighteenth Vow] are those who commit the five grave offenses and slander the true Dharma" (*Dai- muryōjukyō,* T.12:268a, 272b; *Kyōgyōshinshō,* T.83:598b).

Consequently, nenbutsu people especially must not slander other sects. We see, too, that scholars of the various sects of the path of sages should never slander people of the nenbutsu. For although there are many of these passages in the sutras and commentaries, we have been strictly warned about

this, first of all, in the *Commentary on the Mahāprajñāpāramitā Sūtra* by
Nāgārjuna Bodhisattva, the founder of the eight schools. That passage says:
777b "If, out of attachment to the Dharma he follows, a person speaks ill of the
Dharma of others, he will not escape the sufferings of hell, even if he is one
who observes the precepts" (*Daichidoron,* T.25:63c).

Since we have clear testimonials such as this, [we realize that] all are the
Buddha's teachings and that we must not mistakenly slander them. As they
are all relevant to specific sects, the point is surely that we just do not rely
on them; it is outrageous for people in our tradition who have no understanding
to criticize other sects. Those who are head priests in each locality must not
fail to enforce this strictly.

Respectfully.
Bunmei 5 (1473),
the last part of the ninth month.

15. On the Designation
of Our Tradition

Question: How has it come about that there is such a widespread practice of
referring to our tradition as the "Ikkōshū"? I am puzzled about this.

Answer: Our tradition's designation as the "Ikkōshū" was certainly not
determined by our founder. Generally speaking, the reason everyone says
[this] is because we "steadfastly" (*ikkō ni*) rely on Amida Buddha. However,
since a passage in the [*Larger*] *Sutra* teaches "steadfast and exclusive mindfulness of the Buddha of Immeasurable Life" (*Daimuryōjukyō,* T.12:272b),
referring to us as the "Ikkōshū" presents no problem when the implication
is "be steadfastly mindful of the Buddha of Immeasurable Life." Our founder,
however, did indeed designate this sect as the "Jōdo Shinshū." Hence we
know that the term "Ikkōshū" did not come from within our sect. Further,
others within the Jōdoshū allow the sundry practices. Our Master rejected
777c the sundry practices, and it is on this basis that we attain birth in the true and
real (*shinjitsu*) fulfilled land. For this reason, he specifically inserted the character *shin* (true).

A further question: I understand clearly that, long ago, [the founder] designated our tradition as the "Jōdo Shinshū." However, I would like to hear in

detail how it is that in the teaching of our sect, although we are laypeople of deep evil karma, burdened with evil acts and grave offenses, we are to be born readily in the Land of Utmost Bliss through reliance on the working of Amida's Vow.

Answer: The import of our tradition is that when faith is decisively settled, we will unfailingly attain birth in the true and real fulfilled land. And so if you ask what this faith is, [the answer is that] it is just [a matter of] relying single-heartedly and without any worry on Amida Tathāgata, giving no thought to other buddhas and bodhisattvas and entrusting ourselves steadfastly and without any double-mindedness to Amida. This we call "settlement of faith." The two characters *shin-jin* are [literally] read "true mind." We say "true mind" because the practitioner is not saved by his mistaken mind of self-power (*jiriki no kokoro*) but by the right mind of other-power given by the Tathāgata.

Further, we are not saved simply by repeating the Name without any understanding of it. Hence the [*Larger*] *Sutra* teaches that we "hear the Name and realize faith and joy" (*Daimuryōjukyō,* T.12:272b; *Kyōgyōshinshō,* T.83:601a, 605a). "Hearing the Name" is not hearing the six-character Name *na-mu-a-mi-da-butsu* unreflectively; it means that when we meet a good teacher, receive his teaching, and entrust ourselves (*namu*) to the Name (*namu-amida-butsu*), Amida Buddha unfailingly saves us. This is explained in the [*Larger*] *Sutra* as "realizing faith and joy." Consequently, we should understand that *namu-amida-butsu* shows how he saves us.

778a

After we have come to this realization, we must bear in mind that the Name we say walking, standing, sitting, and lying down is simply an expression of gratitude for Amida Tathāgata's benevolence in saving us. With this, we are to be declared other-power nenbutsu practitioners who have attained faith and will be born in the Land of Utmost Bliss.

Respectfully.

The compilation and writing of this letter were completed between 9:00 and 11:00 A.M. on the second day of the latter part of the ninth month, Bunmei 5 (1473), at the hot springs at Yamanaka, Kaga province.

Shōnyo, disciple of Śākyamuni
(written seal)

Fascicle II

1. On Clearing the
Channels of Faith

I hear that during the past seven days of thanksgiving services, wives of the priests in charge of lodgings and others as well have, for the most part, undergone a decisive settling of faith. This is wonderful, and one could hope for nothing more. And yet, if we just let things be, faith, too, will disappear. It does seem that "time after time, [we must] clear the channels of faith and let the waters of Amida's Dharma flow."

In regard to this, [it must be understood that] although women have been abandoned by all the buddhas of the ten directions and the three periods, it is indeed thanks to Amida Tathāgata that they are saved. For to whatever extent women's minds may be true, their inclination to doubt is deep, and their tendency to avoid things [impure and inauspicious] is still more difficult   778b
to cast off. Laywomen in particular, absorbed in practical matters and in their concern for children and grandchildren, devote themselves only to this life; and while they know the human realm—so patently ephemeral—to be a place of uncertainty for young and old alike, they pass their nights and days to no purpose, giving no thought at all to the fact that they will soon sink into the three evil paths and the eight difficulties. This is the way of ordinary people; it is inexpressibly deplorable.

They must, therefore, take refuge singleheartedly and steadfastly in the compassionate vow of the one Amida Buddha and deeply entrust themselves; discarding the inclination to engage in the sundry practices, they must also cast off all thought of courting favor with the *kami* and other buddhas. Then, realizing that Amida Tathāgata made the Primal Vow for the sake of wretched women like themselves and that the Buddha's wisdom is indeed inconceivable, and knowing that they are evil and worthless beings, they should be deeply moved to turn and enter [the mind of] the Tathāgata. Then they will realize that their entrusting [of themselves] and their mindfulness [of Amida] are both brought about through Amida Tathāgata's compassionate means.

59

778c   People who understand [the teaching] in this way are precisely those who have attained other-power faith. Moreover, this state is described as "dwelling in the company of those [whose birth in the Pure Land is] truly settled," "[being certain of] reaching nirvana," "reaching the stage equal to perfect enlightenment," and "[being in] the same [stage] as Maitreya." We also say that these are people whose births have been settled with the awakening of the one thought-moment [of faith]. Bear in mind that, on the basis of this understanding, the nenbutsu (the saying of the Name) is the nenbutsu of joy, expressing our gratitude for the benevolence of Amida Tathāgata who readily settles our birth.

Respectfully.

First of all, observe our tradition's regulations very carefully in regard to the above. For if [people] fully understand the way of faith as stated here, they will store it deep within themselves and not give any sign of it in the presence of those of other sects and others [not of our tradition]; neither will they talk about faith. As for the *kami* [and other buddhas], we simply do not rely on them; we must not belittle them. The Master also spoke of the person who is "true" as described above—in both matters of faith and matters of conduct—as a practitioner of faith who has discretion. Quite simply, we are to be deeply mindful of the buddha-dharma.

Respectfully.

I have written this letter on the eighth day of the twelfth month of Bunmei 5 (1473) and am giving it to the wives of the priests in charge of the lodgings on this mountain. If there are other matters still in question, they should inquire again.

With the passage of winter and summer,
age 58. (seal)

I have written this down
As a guide
For future generations—
May these words on the Dharma
Be my memento.

60

2. On the Point
of Departure

In the school founded by the Master, faith is placed before all else. If we ask 779a
the purpose of that faith, [the answer is that] it is the point of departure enabling
wretched ordinary beings like ourselves, who lack good and do evil, to go
readily to Amida's Pure Land. Without attaining faith, we will not be born in
the Land of Utmost Bliss but will fall into the hell of incessant pain (*avīci*).

If we then ask how to attain that faith, [the answer is that], relying deeply
on the single buddha, Amida Tathāgata, we give no thought to any of the
various good deeds and myriad practices, and, dismissing the inclination to
make petitions to the various buddhas and bodhisattvas just for this life, and
discarding false, erroneous thoughts such as those of self-power, we entrust
ourselves singleheartedly and steadfastly, without double-mindedness, to
Amida; without fail, Amida embraces such people with his all-pervading light
and will not abandon them. Once we have attained faith (*shin*) in this way,
we should bear in mind that the nenbutsu we say at all times, sleeping or waking, expresses our gratitude for the benevolence of Amida who saves us.

Those who understand as explained above are indeed exemplary of what
it is to have attained faith fully according to our tradition. If there are people
who say that there is something else over and above this called "faith," they
are greatly mistaken. We can never accept [such a claim].

Respectfully.

What has been set down in this letter is the right meaning of faith, taught by
Master Shinran of our tradition. Those who thoroughly understand these points 779b
must never discuss anything to do with this faith in the presence of those of
other sects and others [not of our tradition]. Furthermore, we simply do not
rely on any of the other buddhas and bodhisattvas or on the various *kami;* we
must never belittle them. We must recognize that each and every one of the
various *kami* is indeed included within the virtue of Amida, the one buddha.
Without exception, do not disparage any of the various teachings. By [adhering
to] these points, one will be known as a person who carefully observes our
tradition's rules of conduct. Hence the Master said, "Even if you are called a
'cow thief,' do not act in such a way that you are seen as an aspirant for

[buddhahood in] the afterlife, or as a 'good' person, or as a follower of the buddha-dharma; these were his very words. We must practice the nenbutsu, keeping these points very carefully in mind.

Written on the evening of the twelfth day,
the twelfth month, of Bunmei 5 (1473).

3. On Three Items, [Including] *Kami* Manifestations

Within the school of teaching propagated by our tradition's founding Master, there have been discrepancies in what everyone has preached. From now on, therefore—from the priests in charge of the lodgings on this mountain on down to those [priests] who read [but] a single volume of the scriptures, each of the people who assemble [here], and each of those who want to be enrolled as followers of this school—[all] must know the provisions of these three items and henceforth be governed accordingly.

779c   *Item:* Do not slander other teachings and other sects.
     Item: Do not belittle the various *kami* and buddhas and bodhisattvas.
     Item: Receive faith and attain birth in the fulfilled land.

Those who do not observe the points in the above three items and take them as fundamental, storing them deep in their hearts, are to be forbidden access to this mountain [community].

I left the capital in midsummer of the third year of Bunmei and, in the latter part of the seventh month of the same year, occupied a hut in a wind- and wave-lashed place on this mountain. My purpose in staying here over this four-year period has simply been to lead those throughout the Hokuriku who have not undergone a decisive settling of faith according to our tradition into the same faith (*anjin*), [guiding them all] uniformly by what is expressed in these three items. For this reason, I have persevered until now. Therefore if you honor these [items], knowing their significance, this will indeed accomplish my fundamental intent in staying in this region for these months and years.

     Item: By *kami* manifestations, we mean that [buddhas and bodhisattvas] appear provisionally as *kami* to save sentient beings in whatever way possible; they lament that those who lack faith (*shin*) in the buddha-dharma fall helplessly into hell. Relying on even the slightest of [related past] conditions, they appear provisionally as *kami* through compassionate means to lead [sentient beings] at last into the buddha-dharma.

Therefore sentient beings of the present time [should realize that] if they rely on Amida and, undergoing a decisive settling of faith, repeat the nenbutsu and are to be born in the Land of Utmost Bliss, then all the *kami* [in their various] manifestations, recognizing this as [the fulfillment of] their own fundamental purpose, will rejoice and protect nenbutsu practitioners. Consequently, even if we do not worship the *kami* in particular, since all are encompassed when we rely solely on one buddha, Amida, we give credence [to them] even though we do not rely on them in particular.

Item: Within our tradition, there must be no slander of other teachings and other sects. As the teachings were all given by Śākya[muni] during his lifetime, they should be fruitful if they are practiced just as they were expounded. In this last [Dharma] age, however, people like ourselves are not equal to the teachings of the various sects of the path of sages; therefore, we simply do not rely on them or entrust ourselves to them.

Item: Because the buddhas and bodhisattvas are discrete manifestations of Amida Tathāgata, [Amida] is the original teacher and the original buddha of the buddhas of the ten directions. For this reason, when we take refuge in one buddha, Amida, we take refuge in all the buddhas and bodhisattvas; hence the buddhas and bodhisattvas are all encompassed within the one body of Amida.

Item: Amida Tathāgata's true and real other-power faith, taught by our founder Master Shinran, is formalized in our entrusting ourselves to the Primal Vow by discarding all sundry practices and steadfastly and singleheartedly taking refuge in Amida through the single practice [of the nenbutsu] and singlemindedness. Therefore, in accord with what we have heard from our predecessors—bearing in mind continually that Amida Tathāgata's true and real faith is the inconceivable [working] of the Buddha's wisdom that is imparted by other-power, and having determined that the [awakening of the] one thought-moment [of faith] is the

780a

780b

time when birth [in the Pure Land] is assured—[we realize that] it is a matter of course that if one's life continues on after that, there will naturally be many utterances [of the nenbutsu]. Accordingly, we are taught that the many utterances, the [many] callings of the Name, are in grateful return for the Buddha's benevolence, birth [in the Pure Land] being assured in ordinary life with [the awakening of] a single thought-moment [of faith].

Therefore the essential point transmitted by the founding Master in our school is but one thing: this faith. Not knowing this [is what distinguishes those of] other schools; knowing it is the mark of [those who participate in] the Shinshū. Further, in the presence of others [not of our tradition], you must never display outwardly what it is to be a person of the nenbutsu according to this tradition. This is the foundation for the conduct of those who have attained the faith of the Shinshū.

[The above] is as stated previously.

Written on the eleventh day
of the first month of Bunmei 6 (1474).

4. On Severing Crosswise the Five Evil Courses

[*Question:*] The reason why the Primal Vow of Amida Tathāgata is said to be "all-surpassing" is that it is the supreme vow made for the sake of ordinary beings like ourselves who, belonging to the defiled world of the last [Dharma] age, commit evil and lack good. Yet we have no clear understanding as to how we should conceive of this, and how we should entrust ourselves to Amida in order to be born in the Pure Land. Please tell us about this in detail.

Answer: Sentient beings [living] now, in the last [Dharma] age, should simply entrust themselves exclusively to Amida Tathāgata; even though they do not rely on other buddhas and bodhisattvas as well, the Buddha has vowed with great mercy and great compassion that, however deep their evil karma may be, he will save those who singleheartedly and steadfastly take refuge in one buddha, Amida. Sending forth the great light [of his compassion], he receives them within that light. Hence the *Contemplation Sutra* teaches: "The

780c

64

light shines throughout the worlds of the ten directions, and sentient beings mindful of the Buddha are embraced, never to be abandoned" (*Kanmuryō-jukyō*, T.12:343b).

Because of this, the way that will surely lead us to the evil courses, "the five paths" or "the six paths," is closed off through the inconceivable working of Amida Tathāgata's Vow. How this comes about is explained in the *Larger Sutra:* "One severs crosswise the five evil courses, and the evil courses close off of themselves" (*Daimuryōjukyō*, T.12:274b).

Therefore however much we may fear that we are going to fall into hell, when we entrust ourselves without a single thought of doubt to the Tathāgata's Vow, those [of us] who are received into Amida Tathāgata's embracing light will not fall into hell through our designing but are certain to go to the Land of Utmost Bliss. When this has become clear to us, since it is we who receive the immeasurable benevolence of the Tathāgata's great compassion, all we can do—day and night, morning and evening—is to say the nenbutsu in gratitude for the Buddha's benevolence, repeating the Name at all times. This is precisely what it is to have attained true and real faith.

Respectfully.

In the sixth year of Bunmei (1474), the evening of the fifteenth day of the second month, remembering the [day] long ago when the Great Sage, the World-honored One, passed into nirvana. Beneath the lamp, rubbing my weakening eyes, I have finished blackening my brush.

Age 60. (seal)

5. On Devotional Beads

From what I have observed of the ways of nenbutsu people on this mountain over the past three or four years, there is indeed no sign of [anyone] having undergone a decisive settling of the faith (*anjin*) that is other-power. The reason for [my saying] this is that there is no one who even carries devotional 781a beads. It is as if they grasped the Buddha directly with bare hands. The Master certainly never said that we should venerate the Buddha by discarding the beads. Nevertheless, even if we do not carry them, all that is necessary for birth in the Pure Land is simply other-power faith. Given that, there are no obstacles. [Yet] it is well for those of priestly rank to wear robes and carry devotional beads; people who have attained true and real faith unfailingly voice it, and it is evident in their bearing.

At present, then, it seems that those who have properly attained true and real faith are extremely rare. When we ask why this is, we find that, because [priests] do not realize the wonder of Amida Tathāgata's Primal Vow and its suitability for us, they persist in their own thinking in regard to whatever they hear, always pretending that they understand about faith; without really hearing anything, they merely imitate others. Since they are in this state, their own birth in the Land of Utmost Bliss seems uncertain. Needless to say, they cannot possibly teach our followers and companions [in the tradition]. In such a frame of mind as this, birth in the fulfilled land in the afterlife is impossible.

What a deplorable situation! We must simply calm our minds and reflect on this. Indeed, human life may end at any time, whenever the outgoing breath fails to await the incoming of the next. We must by all means take the buddha-dharma carefully into our hearts and let faith be decisively settled.

781b

Respectfully.

Written in haste, early in the morning of the sixteenth day of the second month, in the sixth year of Bunmei (1474).

6. On Norms of Conduct

If there are any of you who have heard the meaning of our tradition's other-power faith and become decisively settled, you must store the truth of that faith in the bottom of your hearts; do not talk about it with those of other sects or others [not of our tradition]. Furthermore, you must not praise it openly [in the presence of such people] on byways and main roads and in the villages where you live. Next, do not slight the provincial military governors and local land stewards, claiming that you have attained faith; meet your public obligations in full without fail. Further, do not belittle the various *kami* and buddhas and bodhisattvas, for they are all encompassed within the six characters *na-mu-a-mi-da-butsu*. Besides this, in particular, take the laws of the state as your outer aspect, store other-power faith deep in your hearts, and take [the principles of] humanity and justice as essential. Bear in mind that these are the rules of conduct that have been established within our tradition.

Respectfully.
Written on the seventeenth day
of the second month of Bunmei 6 (1474).

7. "Going Is Easy, Yet No One Is [Born] There"

On quiet consideration, [we realize that] it is indeed due to the efficacy of keeping the five precepts that we receive life in the human realm. This is an extremely rare event. Nevertheless, life in the human realm is but a momentary passage; the afterlife is the blissful result in eternity. And even if we boast of wealth and enjoy overwhelming fame, it is the way of the world that "those who prosper will surely decline, and those who meet are certain to part"; hence we cannot hold to such prosperity for long. It will last only fifty to a hundred years. When we hear, too, of the uncertainty of life for old and young alike, [we realize that] there is indeed little upon which we can depend. Accordingly, sentient beings of the present [age] should aspire to birth in the Pure Land through other-power faith.

781c

To receive that faith, there is no need at all for wisdom or learning, for wealth and status or for poverty and distress; it does not matter if one is good or evil, male or female. What is fundamental is that we simply discard the sundry practices and take refuge in the right practice. To take refuge in the right practice is just to rely on Amida Tathāgata singleheartedly and steadfastly, without any contriving. Sentient beings everywhere who entrust themselves in this way are embraced within [Amida's] light; he does not abandon them, and when life is spent, he brings them without fail to the Pure Land. It is through this singleminded faith alone that we are born in the Pure Land. How readily we attain this settled mind—there is no effort on our part! Hence the two characters *an-jin* are read "easily [attained] mind"; they have this meaning.

Through faith alone, singleheartedly and steadfastly relying on the Tathāgata, we will be born without any difficulty at all in the Land of Utmost Bliss.

67

This settled mind—how readily we understand it! And the Pure Land—how easily we go there! Hence the *Larger Sutra* teaches: "Going is easy, and yet no one is [born] there" (*Daimuryōjukyō,* T.12:274b). This passage means that when we realize the settled mind and rely steadfastly on Amida, it is

782a   easy to go to the Pure Land; but because those who receive faith are rare, although it is easy to go to the Pure Land, no one is [born] there.

Once we have reached this understanding, the Name we say day and night, morning and evening, is solely an expression of gratitude for the benevolence of the universal vow of great compassion. Deeply mindful of the buddha-dharma and knowing the significance of faith, which is readily received, we will unfailingly attain the birth that is to come in the fulfilled land, which is the matter of greatest importance.

Respectfully.

A fair copy, made on the third day

of the third month, Bunmei 6 (1474).

8. On the Original Teacher and the Original Buddha

People of evil [karma] who have committed the ten transgressions and the five grave offenses and women, burdened with the five obstacles and the three submissions—all of whom have been excluded from the compassionate vows of all the buddhas of the ten directions and the three periods and help-lessly abandoned—these are ordinary beings no different from ourselves. Therefore, since Amida Tathāgata is the original teacher and the original buddha of all the buddhas of the three periods and the ten directions, it was Amida who (as the buddha existing from the distant past) made the all-sur-passing, great Vow: he himself would save all of us sentient beings equally—women, burdened with the five obstacles and the three submissions, and ordinary beings in the last [Dharma] age like [ourselves] who, lacking good, have been abandoned by all the buddhas. Thus making the supreme vow, he became Amida Buddha long ago. Apart from relying exclusively on this tathāgata, there is no way at all for sentient beings in the last [Dharma] age to be born in the Land of Utmost Bliss. Accordingly, those who fully know

other-power faith, which was taught by Master Shinran, are all certain to be   782b
born in the Pure Land, ten people out of ten.

[*Question:*] When we think of receiving faith and going to Amida's fulfilled
land, what should our attitude be, and what should we understand about the
way we receive this faith? I would like to hear about this in detail.

Answer: The meaning of other-power faith as taught by Master Shinran
in our tradition is that when we simply realize that we are wretched beings
of deep evil karma, entrust ourselves singleheartedly and steadfastly to Amida
Tathāgata, discard the sundry practices, and devote ourselves to "the single
practice and singlemindedness," we will be received without fail within
[Amida's] all-pervading light. This is indeed how birth [in the Pure Land]
is decisively settled.

Above and beyond this, what we must bear in mind is that, once birth is
assured through the one thought-moment of faith in which we singleheartedly
and steadfastly take refuge in Amida, the Name that we say walking, standing,
sitting, and lying down is the nenbutsu of gratitude [said in] return for the
benevolence of Amida Tathāgata's great compassion in readily settling our
birth. This you should know. In other words, this is [the frame of mind of]
a person who is decisively settled in our tradition's faith.

Respectfully.
The middle of the third month, Bunmei 6 (1474).

9. On "The Loyal Retainer
and the Faithful Wife"

Why is it that, in relying on Amida Tathāgata, we completely reject the myriad
good deeds and practices, designating them as the sundry practices? It is   782c
[because of] the great Vow, in which Amida Buddha has promised to save
sentient beings who rely on him singleheartedly and steadfastly, however
deep their evil karma may be. Therefore, "singleheartedly and steadfastly"
means that we take no other buddha as peer to Amida Buddha. This is the
same as the rule in human society that one relies on only one master. Hence,
in the words of an outer [non-Buddhist] text, "a loyal retainer will not serve
two masters; a faithful wife will not take a second husband." Since Amida

Tathāgata is the original teacher and master of all the buddhas of the three periods, how can all the buddhas who are his disciples not rejoice when we rely on that buddha who is the master? You must understand the grounds for this very thoroughly.

Since the substance of practice, *namu-amida-butsu,* encompasses all the *kami,* buddhas, and bodhisattvas and, besides these, each and every one of the myriad good deeds and practices, what could be lacking that would necessitate our putting our minds to the various practices and good deeds? The Name *namu-amida-butsu* completely embodies all the myriad good deeds and practices; hence it is surely trustworthy.

Then how do we rely on Amida Tathāgata and how do we entrust ourselves and attain birth in the Land of Utmost Bliss?

783a

There is no need for effort on our part; when we just realize deeply that Amida Tathāgata himself graciously made the Vow to save those of us who, as wretched beings burdened with the most deeply rooted evil, can only go to hell, and when faith is awakened in the one thought-moment of taking refuge, then—surely prompted by the unfolding of past good as well—other-power faith is granted through the wisdom of the Buddha. Consequently, the Buddha's mind and the mind of the ordinary being become one; the person who has attained such a state of mind is called a practitioner who has attained faith. Beyond this, we must bear in mind that, simply by saying the nenbutsu, sleeping or waking, no matter where or when, we should express our gratitude for the benevolence of the universal vow of great compassion.

Respectfully.

Written on the seventeenth day
of the third month, Bunmei 6 (1474).

10. On the Oneness of the Buddha's Mind and the Mind of Ordinary Beings

[*Question:*] The import of the basic principles taught by Master Shinran of our tradition is, first of all, that other-power faith is of the utmost importance. It is clearly seen in the sutras and commentaries that, without fully knowing this other-power faith, [realization of] the birth that is to come in the Land of Utmost Bliss—the matter of greatest importance—is indeed not possible. Therefore when we know what other-power faith is all about and aspire to birth in the true and real fulfilled land, what should our attitude be, and what should we do to attain birth in this Land of Utmost Bliss? I do not know about this in any detail. Please let me have your kind instruction. I feel that after hearing this, I shall surely attain firm faith.

Answer: The import of other-power faith in our tradition is that, without worrying at all about the depth of our evil karma, we simply entrust ourselves singleheartedly and steadfastly to Amida Tathāgata and realize deeply that it is indeed the inconceivable power of the Vow that saves everyone—people of evil [karma] (like ourselves) who have committed the ten transgressions and the five grave offenses, and even women burdened with the five obstacles and the three submissions; and when there is not a moment's doubt of the Primal Vow, the Tathāgata, fully knowing that [practitioner's] mind, graciously causes the evil mind of the practitioner to be entirely the same as the good mind of the Tathāgata. This is what is meant by our saying that "the Buddha's mind and the mind of the ordinary being become one." Consequently, we should realize that we have been received within Amida Tathāgata's all-pervading light and that we will dwell within this light for the duration of our lives. Then, when life is spent, [Amida] brings us at once to the true and real fulfilled land.

783b

How, then, do we respond to the gracious, inestimable benevolence of Amida's great compassion? [The answer is that] by simply repeating the nenbutsu, saying the Name of the Buddha—day and night, morning and evening—we express our gratitude for Amida Tathāgata's benevolence. Bear in mind that this is what is meant by the teaching of "completing the cause [of birth] in ordinary life, with the awakening of the one thought-moment [of entrusting]," as set forth in our tradition. Therefore, in relying singleheartedly on Amida in this way, there is no need for special effort on our part. As it is easy to receive faith, it is easier still to become a buddha—to be born in the Land of Utmost Bliss. How precious Amida's Primal Vow is! How precious other-power faith is! There is no doubt at all as to our birth.

Yet, beyond this, there is a further point that should be clearly understood in regard to our conduct. That is, all the *kami* and buddhas have appeared as the various *kami* and buddhas through compassionate means, to enable us to

783c

71

receive this singular other-power faith that we realize now. Therefore, because all the [*kami*], buddhas, and bodhisattvas are originally discrete manifestations of Amida Tathāgata, all—each and every one—are encompassed within the single thought-moment in which we, entrusting ourselves, say *Namu-amida-butsu;* for this reason, we are not to belittle them.

Again, there is still another point to be understood. You must never slight the provincial military governors and local land stewards, saying that you are a person who reveres the buddha-dharma and has attained faith. Meet your public obligations in full without fail.

People who comply with the above exemplify the conduct of nenbutsu practitioners in whom faith has been awakened and who aspire to [birth in the Pure Land in] the afterlife. They are, in other words, ones who faithfully abide by the buddha-dharma and the laws of the state.

Respectfully.

Written on the thirteenth day
of the fifth month, Bunmei 6 (1474).

11. On the Fivefold Teaching

In recent years, the import of the teaching of our tradition's Master Shinran has been presented in various ways in the provinces, with a lack of uniformity. This is a most deplorable situation. For, to begin with, although the birth of ordinary beings [in the Pure Land] through other-power faith has been of primary importance in our tradition, [some] brush aside the matter of faith and do not consider it. They propose that "faith is not forgetting that Amida Tathā-gata settled our birth at the time of his perfect enlightenment ten *kalpa*s ago." What is completely lacking in this is the element of taking refuge in Amida and realizing other-power faith. Therefore however well they may know that their birth has been settled since the time of [Amida's] perfect enlightenment ten *kalpa*s ago, unless they fully know the significance of other-power faith, through which we attain birth, they will not attain birth in the Land of Utmost Bliss. There are also some people who say, "Even if we take refuge in Amida, this is to no avail without a good teacher. Therefore, there is nothing for us

784a

72

to do but rely on a good teacher." These are their words. They, too, are people who have not properly attained our tradition's faith.

The function of a good teacher is just to encourage people to take refuge in Amida singleheartedly and steadfastly. Therefore a fivefold teaching has been established [giving the conditions necessary for birth]: first, [the unfolding of] good from the past; second, [meeting] a good teacher; third, [encountering Amida's] light; fourth, [attaining] faith; and, fifth, [saying] the Name [of the Buddha]. Unless this fivefold teaching is realized, it is evident [in the received texts] that birth is impossible. Thus the good teacher is the messenger who tells us to take refuge in Amida Buddha. Without meeting a good teacher through the unfolding of good from the past, birth is impossible. Bear in mind, however, that to abandon Amida, in whom we take refuge, and to take only the good teacher as essential is a serious error.

Respectfully.

Bunmei 6 (1474), 5.20   784b

12. On the Fifty Years
of Human Life

When we consider the fifty years of human life, [we realize that] they correspond to a day and a night in the heaven of the four kings. Moreover, fifty years in the heaven of the four kings is but a day and a night in the hell of repeated existence. Despite this fact, people take no notice of falling into hell and undergoing suffering; neither do they think deeply of going to the Pure Land and enjoying unsurpassed bliss. Thus they live to no purpose and, passing days and months in vain, pay no attention to the decisive settling of the one mind of their own [faith]. They never look at a single volume of the scriptures, nor do they ever instruct their followers by citing a single passage of the teachings. Morning and evening, they simply watch for spare moments, stretch out with their pillows, and go off to sleep. Surely this is deplorable. Think it over quietly.

From now on, therefore, those who in their negligence fail to uphold the Dharma must by all means seek to attain birth in the true and real fulfilled land through the decisive settling of faith; this will indeed bring benefit to them. It should be recognized, moreover, that this is in accord with the principle of benefiting oneself and benefiting others.

Respectfully.

This was written on the second day of the middle period of the sixth month, Bunmei 6 (1474). I have simply let words flow from the brush in the extreme heat.

13. On the Reputation of Our School

784c
Fully observing the regulations established in our tradition means acting in such a way toward other sects and toward society that we do not draw public attention to our sect; we take this as fundamental. Recently, however, there have been some among the nenbutsu people in our tradition who have deliberately brought to others' notice what our school is all about; they have thought that this would enhance the reputation of our school and, in particular, they have sought to denigrate other schools. Nothing could be more absurd. Moreover, it deeply contradicts Master [Shinran]'s intention. For he said precisely, long ago, "Even if you are called a 'cow thief,' do not give the appearance of [being a participant in] our tradition." We must keep these words very carefully in mind.

Next, those who seek to know in full what settled mind means in our tradition need no wisdom or learning at all; they do not need to be male or female, noble or humble. For when we simply realize that we are wretched beings of deep evil karma and know that the only buddha who saves even such persons as this is Amida Tathāgata, and when, without any contriving, but with the thought of holding fast to the sleeve of this Amida Buddha, we entrust ourselves [to him] to save us, [bringing us to buddhahood] in the afterlife, then Amida Tathāgata deeply rejoices and, sending forth from himself eighty-four thousand great rays of light, receives us within that light. This is clearly explained in the [*Contemplation*] *Sutra:* "The light shines throughout the worlds of the ten directions, and sentient beings mindful of the Buddha are embraced, never to be abandoned" (*Kanmuryōjukyō,* T.12:343b). This
785a
you should know.

74

There is, then, no worry about becoming a buddha. How incomparable is the all-surpassing Primal Vow! And how gracious is Amida Tathāgata's light! Without encountering the [receptive] condition of this light, there can be no cure at all for the fearful sickness of ignorance and karma-hindrance which has been ours from the beginningless past. Yet now, prompted by the condition of this light, good from the past comes into being, and we assuredly attain other-power faith. It is immediately clear, however, that this is faith granted by Amida Tathāgata. Thus we now know beyond question that this is not faith generated by the practitioner but that it is Amida Tathāgata's great other-power faith. Accordingly, all those who have once attained other-power faith should reflect deeply on how gracious Amida Tathāgata's benevolence is and repeat the nenbutsu, saying the Name of the Buddha always in gratitude for the Buddha's benevolence.

Respectfully.
Written on the third day
of the seventh month, Bunmei 6 (1474).

14. On "Secret Teachings"

The "secret teachings" that are widespread in Echizen province are certainly not the buddha-dharma; they are deplorable, outer [non-Buddhist] teachings. Relying on them is futile; it creates karma through which one sinks for a long time into the hell of incessant pain (avīci). You must never, never follow those who are still attached to these secret [teachings] and who, considering them to be of the utmost importance, ingratiate themselves with others and deceive them. Separate yourself immediately from those who expound secret [teachings], lose no time in confessing them just as you have received them, and warn everyone about them. 785b

Those who seek to know thoroughly the meaning of our tradition's teaching and be born in the Land of Utmost Bliss must, to begin with, know about other-power faith. What is the importance of other-power faith?

It is the provision by which wretched ordinary beings like ourselves go readily to the Pure Land.

In what way does other-power faith find expression?

We simply entrust ourselves exclusively to Amida Tathāgata, singleheartedly and steadfastly, without any contriving. And with the awakening of the one thought-moment in which we realize that Amida saves us, Amida Tathāgata unfailingly sends forth his embracing light and keeps us safe within this light as long as we are in this [sahā] world. It is precisely in this state that our birth is assured.

Thus *namu-amida-butsu* expresses the attainment of other-power faith. We should bear in mind that this faith expresses the significance of *namu-amida-butsu*. Then, because we receive this one other-power faith, there is no doubt at all that we will be born readily in the Land of Utmost Bliss.

785c   How incomparable is Amida Tathāgata's other-power Primal Vow! How are we to respond to this gracious benevolence of Amida? Simply by saying *Namu-amida-butsu, Namu-amida-butsu,* sleeping or waking, we respond to Amida Tathāgata's benevolence. With what mind, then, do we say *Namu-amida-butsu?*

Think of it as the rejoicing mind that realizes, with humility and wonder, the graciousness of Amida Tathāgata's saving work.

Respectfully.

Bunmei 6 (1474), 7.5

15. On Kubon and Chōrakuji

(Hōnen)

[Anjin]

In Japan, various branches of the Jōdo sect have been established; it is divided into Seizan, Chinzei, Kubon, Chōrakuji, and many others. Although the teaching set forth by Master Hōnen is one, when some people who had been followers of the path of sages came to the master and listened to the Pure Land teaching, they did not properly understand his explanation; because of this, still not having given up the ways of their original sects, they tried instead to bring these into the Jōdoshū. Consequently, there is a lack of uniformity. Nevertheless, we must never slander these [ways]. What is important is simply that we store our sect's faith (*anjin*) deep in our minds and, with our own [faith] decisively settled, exhort others as well.

What is the meaning of faith (*anjin*) within our tradition?

[The answer is that,] first of all, being deeply convinced that we are worthless beings burdened with the ten transgressions and the five grave offenses, the five obstacles and the three submissions, we then recognize that it is the inconceivable working of Amida Tathāgata's Primal Vow that, as its primary aim, saves just such wretched persons; and when we deeply entrust ourselves and have not the slightest doubt, Amida embraces [us] without fail. This is precisely what it is to have attained true and real other-power faith. In realizing faith in this way, with [the awakening of] the one thought-moment [of entrusting], there is no need for any effort on our part.

786a

This other-power faith—how readily we can understand it! And the Name [of the Buddha]—how readily we can practice it! Realizing faith is therefore nothing other than this, and understanding the six characters *na-mu-a-mi-da-butsu* is the substance of other-power faith.

What is the meaning of *namu-amida-butsu?* The two characters *na-mu* mean that, aspiring for birth in the Land of Utmost Bliss, we deeply entrust ourselves to Amida. Then Amida Buddha takes pity on sentient beings who entrust themselves in this way, and although ours is an existence burdened with terrible offenses for myriads of *kalpa*s from the beginningless past, because we encounter the [receptive] condition of Amida Tathāgata's light, all the deep offenses of ignorance and karma-hindrance are immediately extinguished, and we assuredly dwell among those [whose birth is] truly settled. Then, discarding the ordinary body, we attain the buddha body. This is what "Amida Tathāgata" signifies. It is on these grounds that the three characters *a-mi-da* are read "receives, saves, and delivers."

Once faith has been decisively settled in this way, if we then realize the graciousness of Amida Tathāgata's benevolence and simply repeat the nenbutsu, saying the Name of the Buddha, that will truly fulfill the principle of responding in gratitude to Amida Tathāgata's benevolence.

786b

Respectfully.
Written on the ninth day
of the seventh month, Bunmei 6 (1474).

Shōnyo, disciple of Śākyamuni
(written seal)

Fascicle III

1. On People Who Are
Only Listed by Name

People who are only listed by name in our tradition as well as those who have been followers for a long time [should realize that] if they do not fully understand what the settled mind is, they must by all means, from this day on, carefully inquire of others about the great faith that is other-power, so that their birth in the fulfilled land may be decisively settled. Realizing the settled mind in our tradition is simply [a matter of] relying deeply and exclusively on Amida Tathāgata. But what sort of buddha is this Amida Buddha, and what sort of person does he save?

It was Amida Buddha who made the great Vow that he alone would save us ordinary beings and women, wretched and abandoned by all the buddhas of the three periods. He meditated for five *kalpa*s and, undergoing practices for numberless *kalpa*s, vowed to save even those sentient beings whose evil karma includes the ten transgressions and the five grave offenses, those who slander the Dharma, and those who lack the seed of buddhahood (*icchantika*). Surpassing the compassionate vows of the various buddhas, he completely fulfilled this Vow and thus became Amida Tathāgata (whom we know also   786c
as Amida Buddha).

Then how do we entrust ourselves to this buddha, and what frame of mind should we have to be saved?

[The answer is that] we disregard the depth of our evil karma and simply entrust ourselves to Amida Buddha steadfastly and without double-mindedness; and when we are completely free of doubt, he will save us without fail.

Amida Tathāgata, then, assuredly delivers all sentient beings by two means, "embracing" and "light." First of all, when those with good from the past are illumined by this light, the evil that has accumulated as karma-hindrances is all extinguished. Then, as for "embracing," since all evil hindrances are extinguished when we encounter the [receptive] condition of this light, sentient beings are immediately received within it. Hence these two, "embracing" and "light," are of the utmost importance in Amida Buddha's [saving work].

In saying that faith is settled with [the awakening of] the one thought-moment of taking refuge [in Amida], we mean that it is when we encounter this embracing light that the settling of faith occurs. It is clear at this present time, therefore, that the substance of practice, *namu-amida-butsu,* expresses in six characters precisely how it is that we are to be born in the Pure Land. Knowing this, I am more and more thankful and filled with awe.

787a   Then, once faith is decisively settled, we should—sleeping or waking—just say the nenbutsu in gratitude, joyfully remembering that we have received Amida Tathāgata's benevolence beyond measure. That is indeed the practice that truly returns the Buddha's benevolence.

Respectfully.

Written on the fourteenth day
of the seventh month, Bunmei 6 (1474).

2. On Practicing
as Prescribed

The teachings of the various sects differ, but since they were all [expounded] during Śākya[muni]'s lifetime, they are indeed the incomparable Dharma. For this reason, there is absolutely no doubt that people who practice them as prescribed will attain enlightenment and become buddhas. However, sentient beings of this last [Dharma] age are of the lowest capacity; this is a time when those who practice as prescribed are rare.

Here [we realize that] Amida Tathāgata's Primal Vow of other-power was made to save sentient beings in such times as these. To this end, [Amida] meditated for five *kalpa*s and, performing practices for numberless *kalpa*s, vowed that he would not attain perfect enlightenment unless sentient beings who commit evil and lack good reach buddhahood. Completely fulfilling that Vow, he became Amida Buddha. Sentient beings of this last [Dharma] age can never become buddhas unless they deeply entrust themselves to Amida, relying on this buddha's Primal Vow.

How do we entrust ourselves to Amida Tathāgata's other-power Primal Vow, and what frame of mind should we have to be saved?

Entrusting ourselves to Amida simply means that those who truly know 787b what other-power faith is will all be born in the Land of Utmost Bliss, ten people out of ten.

Then what is that other-power faith?

It is simply *namu-amida-butsu*. Fully knowing the meaning of the six characters *na-mu-a-mi-da-butsu* is precisely what other-power faith is all about. We must, therefore, thoroughly understand the substance of these six characters.

To begin with, what do the two characters *na-mu* mean?

Na-mu means relying on Amida singleheartedly and steadfastly, without any contriving, and entrusting ourselves without double-mindedness [to Amida] to save us, [bringing us to buddhahood] in the afterlife.

Then, what do the four characters *a-mi-da-butsu* mean?

A-mi-da-butsu means that, without fail, Amida sends forth from himself light that illumines sentient beings who rely on him singleheartedly and are free of doubt, as explained above. He receives them within that light, and when their span of life comes to an end, he brings them to the Pure Land of Utmost Bliss. This is *a-mi-da-butsu*.

According to what is commonly said about the nenbutsu, people think they will be saved if they just repeat *Namu-amida-butsu* with their lips. That is uncertain. There are, however, some within the Jōdo school who teach this. 787c Let us not judge it as right or wrong. I simply explain our tradition's way of faith (*anjin*), which was taught by the founder of our sect. Those who have [good] conditions from the past should hear this and promptly attain [assurance of] the birth that is to come in the Land of Utmost Bliss. Those who understand this should say the Name of the Buddha; [remembering] the benevolence of Amida Tathāgata who readily saves us, they should repeat the nenbutsu, saying the Name of the Buddha in grateful return for the Buddha's benevolence, which we receive beyond measure.

Respectfully.
Written on the fifth day
of the eighth month, Bunmei 6 (1474).

81

3. On the Followers of
[the Priest] Shōkō

Concerning the followers of [the priest] Shōkō of Kawajiri in this region: I cannot but feel uneasy about their understanding of faith according to the buddha-dharma. I shall now, however, discuss our tradition's basic principles in detail. Each person should listen to this attentively, take it as fundamental, and thus be assured of the birth that is to come in the Land of Utmost Bliss.

What does "Amida Tathāgata's Primal Vow of birth through the nenbutsu" mean?

[The answer is that] if only other-power faith is decisively settled, laypeople lacking wisdom and even those who have committed the ten transgressions and the five grave offenses will all be born in the Land of Utmost Bliss.

How difficult is it, then, to attain that faith?

Those who, without any worry, simply entrust themselves exclusively (with no double-mindedness) to Amida Tathāgata and keep their thoughts from straying in other directions will all become buddhas, ten people out of ten. It is easy to hold to this single mind [of faith]. People who merely repeat the nenbutsu aloud have only a partial understanding; they will not be born in the Land of Utmost Bliss. It is those who fully realize the significance of this nenbutsu who will become buddhas. If only the single thought of fully entrusting ourselves to Amida is settled, we will go readily to the Pure Land.

Besides this, remember that it is outrageous to cite complicated secret [teachings] and not reverence the Buddha.

And so, because Amida Tathāgata's other-power Primal Vow is meant to save people of deep evil karma in this last [Dharma] age, it is the Primal Vow of other-power that is completely suited to laypeople like ourselves. How thankful I am for Amida Tathāgata's Vow! And how thankful I am for Śākya[muni] Tathāgata's golden words! Revere them. Entrust yourselves to them. For those who understand as I have explained above truly exemplify the nenbutsu practitioner in whom our tradition's faith is decisively settled.

Then, beyond this, remember that the nenbutsu we say throughout our lives expresses our gratitude for the measureless benevolence of Amida Tathāgata who readily saves us.

788a

Respectfully.
Written on the sixth day   788b
of the eighth month, Bunmei 6 (1474).

4. On the Great Sage, the
World-honored One

When we carefully consider the ephemeral nature of human life, we realize
that the living inevitably face death and that the prosperous eventually decline.
And so we only live out our years, spending nights to no purpose and days
to no avail. This is indeed inexpressibly sad. What is difficult to escape, then,
is impermanence—whether at the highest level, that of the Great Sage, the
World-honored One [Śākyamuni], or at the lowest, that of Devadatta, who
committed transgressions and evil offenses. Now what is extremely difficult
to receive is human form; what is difficult to meet is the buddha-dharma.
Even though we may chance to meet the buddha-dharma, the way leading
to emancipation from birth and death by the path of self-power practices is,
at the present time, in the last [Dharma] age, difficult and beyond our reach.
Because of this, our lives will pass by in vain unless we encounter the Primal
Vow of Amida Tathāgata.

Now, however, we are able to meet the single teaching of the universal vow.
Therefore the only thing we should aspire to is [birth in] the Pure Land of utmost
bliss, and the only one we should rely upon is Amida Tathāgata; with faith decisively settled, we should say the nenbutsu. But what ordinary people generally
have in mind is that if they merely repeat *Namu-amida-butsu* aloud, they will
be born in the Land of Utmost Bliss. That is most uncertain.

What, then, is the meaning of the six characters *na-mu-a-mi-da-butsu?*

We must realize that when anyone relies steadfastly on Amida Tathāgata,
the Buddha saves him, fully knowing that sentient being. This is what is
expressed in the six characters *na-mu-a-mi-da-butsu.*   788c

Then, in order to be saved in [regard to] the most important matter, the
afterlife, how do we entrust ourselves to Amida Tathāgata?

[The answer is that] when we entrust ourselves without any worry or double-mindedness—casting away all sundry practices and miscellaneous good

acts and relying on Amida Tathāgata singleheartedly and steadfastly—[Amida] sends forth his light and embraces within it the sentient beings who rely on him. This is called "receiving the benefit of Amida Tathāgata's embracing light." It is also called "[receiving] the benefit of the vow that never abandons us." Once we have been received in this way within Amida Tathāgata's light, we will be born immediately into the true and real fulfilled land when life is spent. Let there be no doubt about this.

Besides this, what good would it do to rely on other buddhas or to perform meritorious good deeds? How wonderful and gracious Amida Tathāgata is! How can we express our gratitude for this measureless benevolence?

Understand that it is simply by saying aloud *Namu-amida-butsu, Namu-amida-butsu* that we return the [Buddha's] benevolence in profound gratitude.

Respectfully.
Bunmei 6 (1474), 8.18

5. On the Compassionate Vows of Other Buddhas

When we inquire in detail as to why it is that Amida's Primal Vow surpasses the compassionate vows of other buddhas, [we realize that] the buddhas of the ten directions are unable to save sentient beings with extremely deep evil karma or women, who are burdened with the five obstacles and the three submissions. Hence it is said that Amida Buddha's Primal Vow surpasses other buddhas' vows.

What sort of sentient beings does Amida Tathāgata's all-surpassing great Vow save?

It is the great Vow that, without exception, saves evildoers who have committed the ten transgressions and the five grave offenses, and even women, who are burdened with the five obstacles and the three submissions. Hence it is [through] the working of the great Vow of other-power that [Amida] proclaims that he will unfailingly lead to the Land of Utmost Bliss [all] sentient beings, ten people out of ten, who singleheartedly and steadfastly entrust themselves to him.

[*Question:*] Then how do wretched ordinary beings like ourselves rely on Amida Buddha's Primal Vow, and in what frame of mind should we entrust

789a

84

ourselves to Amida? Please explain in detail. Attaining faith according to this teaching, we shall entrust ourselves to Amida, aspire to [birth in] the Land of Utmost Bliss, and say the nenbutsu.

Answer: To begin with, what is now widely taught about the nenbutsu makes people think they will be saved if they merely repeat *Namu-amida-butsu* without any understanding. That is very doubtful. The teaching of the Jōdoshū is divided into various schools in the capital and the provinces. We do not, however, judge that as right or wrong. We simply explain our founder's teaching as it has been transmitted within the tradition.

Now, listen carefully, with the ears of one aspiring to emancipation and with your heads lowered in reverence. You may realize the thought of faith and joy.   789b

Laypeople and those who have committed evil all through their lives should simply disregard the depth of their evil karma and deeply accept Amida Tathāgata's Primal Vow as the inconceivable vow-power centered on saving just such wretched beings [as themselves]. Relying singleheartedly and steadfastly on Amida, they should solely seek to attain other-power faith.

What, then, is other-power faith?

The six-character Name *na-mu-a-mi-da-butsu* shows how it is that Amida Buddha saves us. We say that a person who has understood this in detail is one who has attained other-power faith. The two characters *na-mu* signify sentient beings' entrusting themselves to Amida Buddha singleheartedly and steadfastly, with no other thought than that he will save them. This is called "taking refuge." Next, the four characters *a-mi-da-butsu* signify that, without exception, Amida Buddha saves sentient beings who entrust themselves (*na-mu*). This means, in other words, that he "embraces and never abandons us." "Embraces and never abandons" means that Amida Tathāgata receives nen-butsu practitioners within his light and will not forsake them. And so, in regard to the import of *namu-amida-butsu,* we know that it is in testimony   789c to Amida Buddha's saving us that the Name is expressed in these six characters, *na-mu-a-mi-da-butsu.* When we have understood them in this way, we are assured of birth in the Land of Utmost Bliss.

How gracious and wonderful this is! And beyond this, since we have been saved once and for all by Amida Tathāgata, the nenbutsu expresses the joy of having been saved. Hence we describe this nenbutsu as "the saying of the

Name in gratitude for the Buddha's benevolence" and "the saying of the Name after [the realization of] faith (*shin*)."

Respectfully.
Written on the sixth day
of the ninth month, Bunmei 6 (1474).

6. On Saying the Tathāgata's Name Only, at All Times

What is the meaning of *namu-amida-butsu*?

To begin with, the two characters *na-mu* have two meanings, "to take refuge" and "to aspire to be born and to direct virtue." Also, *namu* is the vow; *amida-butsu* is the practice. When we cast away the sundry practices and miscellaneous good acts and entrust ourselves to Amida Tathāgata with the single practice and singlemindedness, awakening the one thought-moment of taking refuge in which we realize that he saves us, [Amida] graciously sends forth his all-pervading light and receives us. This is precisely what is meant by the four characters *a-mi-da-butsu* and, also, by "aspiring to be born and directing virtue." We see, then, that the six characters *na-mu-a-mi-da-butsu* comprise the Name that fully expresses the significance of other-power faith, through which we are to be born [in the Pure Land].

For this reason, the passage on the fulfillment of the Vow [in the *Larger Sutra*] teaches that we "hear the Name and realize faith and joy" (*Daimuryō-jukyō,* T.12:272b; *Kyōgyōshinshō,* T.83:601a, 605a). The meaning of this passage is that, hearing the Name, we rejoice in faith. "Hearing the Name" is not just hearing it in a general way. It should be understood that when we have met a good teacher and heard and fully realized the significance of the six characters *na-mu-a-mi-da-butsu,* this realization is other-power faith, through which we are to be born in the fulfilled land. Hence "realize faith and joy" means that when faith is settled, we rejoice, knowing that birth in the Pure Land is assured.

790a

And so, when we reflect on Amida Tathāgata's painstaking endeavors for five *kalpa*s [of meditation] and numberless, uncountable *kalpa*s [of practice], and when we think of the graciousness and wonder of his saving us so readily, it is hard to express our feelings. [Shinran] refers to this in a hymn (*Shōzōmatsu wasan,* T.83:666b):

The benevolence of *namu-amida-butsu,* [Amida's] directing of virtue,
    is vast and inconceivable;
As the benefit of his directing virtue toward our going [to the Pure
    Land],
We are led into his directing [virtue] toward our return to this world.

Also, in the *Gāthā of True Faith,* there is [the following passage] (*Shō-shinge,* T.83:600b):

Saying the Tathāgata's Name only, at all times,
We should respond in gratitude to the universal vow of great
    compassion.

Hence [we realize] all the more that—walking, standing, sitting, and lying
down, irrespective of time, place, or any other circumstances—we should
simply repeat the nenbutsu, saying the Name of the Buddha in grateful return
for the Buddha's benevolence.

Respectfully.
Written on the twentieth day
of the tenth month, Bunmei 6 (1474).

7. On the Three Acts of
the Buddha and of
Sentient Beings

What Master Shinran emphasized above all else was other-power faith, the
single path by which lay practitioners in the defiled world of the last [Dharma]
age, lacking wisdom, are born promptly and without difficulty in the Pure Land;
this he taught as fundamental. Everyone knows very well, then, that Amida
Tathāgata unfailingly saves each and every one of the people of utter foolishness
who have committed the ten transgressions and the five grave offenses and even
women burdened with the five obstacles and the three submissions. But how   790b
do we ordinary beings entrust ourselves to Amida Buddha, and in what way do
we rely on him now in order to be born in the world of utmost bliss?

[The answer is that] we simply entrust ourselves exclusively to Amida
Tathāgata and, casting off all other [practices], steadfastly take refuge in

Amida; and when we singleheartedly entrust ourselves to the Primal Vow without double-mindedness in regard to Amida Tathāgata, then, without fail, we will be born in the Land of Utmost Bliss. This is precisely what it is to have attained other-power faith.

Faith is [a matter of] clearly discerning the significance of Amida Buddha's Primal Vow and singleheartedly taking refuge in Amida; this we call decisive settlement of other-power faith (*anjin*). Therefore, full realization of the significance of the six characters *na-mu-a-mi-da-butsu* is the substance of decisively settled faith. That is, the two characters *na-mu* indicate the receptive attitude of the sentient beings, the persons to be saved, who entrust themselves to Amida Buddha. Next, the four characters *a-mi-da-butsu* signify the Dharma through which Amida Tathāgata saves sentient beings. This is expressed as "the oneness in *namu-amida-butsu* of the person [to be saved] and Dharma [that saves]." Thus the three acts of sentient beings and the three acts of Amida become one. Referring to this, Master Shandao wrote in his commentary, "The three acts of the Buddha and of sentient beings are inseparable" (*Kangyōsho,* T.37:268a).

There should be no doubt at all, therefore, that those in whom faith is decisively settled with the one thought-moment of taking refuge will all be born without fail in the fulfilled land. Those who cast off the evil on their side, which is attachment to self-power, and rely singleheartedly on Amida, deeply entrusting themselves and realizing that this is the inconceivable working of the Vow, will all unfailingly attain birth in the true and real fulfilled land, ten people out of ten. Once [we have understood] this, we should say the nenbutsu in gratitude at all times, mindful only of Amida Tathāgata's deep benevolence.

790c

Respectfully.

Bunmei 7 (1475), 2.23

8. On the False "Ten *Kalpas*" Teaching in This Province and Others

In this province and others, [there are many] these days who are sharply at variance with what our tradition teaches about the settled mind. Each person feels that he understands correctly, and few think of making further effort to attain true and real faith by asking others about views that run counter to the Dharma. This is indeed a deplorable attachment. Unless the birth that is to come in the fulfilled land is decisively settled by their quickly repenting and confessing these views and abiding in our tradition's true and real faith, it is indeed just as if they went to a mountain of treasure and returned empty-handed. They say, in words that are at variance with this faith, "Faith is not forgetting or doubting at present that Amida Tathāgata completely settled our birth at the time of his perfect enlightenment ten *kalpa*s ago." Dwelling in this mistaken view—without taking refuge in Amida and having their faith decisively settled—they cannot be born in the fulfilled land. This is, therefore, a deviant and mistaken understanding.

If we are to clarify what the settled mind is in our tradition, we say that to understand *namu-amida-butsu* fully is to have attained other-power faith. Hence Shandao explains the six characters *na-mu-a-mi-da-butsu* by saying, "*Namu* means 'to take refuge.' It also signifies aspiring to be born and directing virtue" (*Kangyōsho,* T.37:250a; *Kyōgyōshinshō,* T.83:594c). 791a

What does this mean?

[The explanation is that] when Amida Tathāgata in his causal stage [as the *bhikṣu* Dharmākara] determined the practice through which we ordinary beings are to be born [in the Pure Land], he labored on our behalf because ordinary beings' directing of virtue is based on self-power and is therefore difficult to accomplish. In order to give this virtue to us, he fulfilled [the practice] through which virtue is directed; he gives it to us ordinary beings with the [awakening of the] one thought-moment of our taking refuge—*namu.* Consequently, this is not a directing of virtue from the side of ordinary beings but the Tathāgata's directing of virtue, which we call a nondirecting of virtue from the practitioner's side. Thus the two characters *na-mu* mean "to take refuge"; they also mean "to aspire for birth and to direct virtue." On these grounds, [Amida] unfailingly embraces and never abandons sentient beings who take refuge (*namu*). For this reason, we say *Namu-amida-butsu.*

This is precisely what we mean when we refer to nenbutsu practitioners who have attained other-power faith through the one thought-moment of taking refuge and who have completed the cause [of birth] in ordinary life. This you should know. People who understand in this way should repeat the nenbutsu, saying the Name of the Buddha [at all times]—walking, standing, sitting, and lying down—truly, acknowledging Amida Tathāgata's deep and boundless benevolence. [Shinran] expresses this in the [following] lines (*Kyōgyōshinshō*, T.83:600b):

> The moment we are mindful of Amida's Primal Vow,
> We are naturally brought to enter the stage of the definitely settled;
> Saying the Tathāgata's Name only, at all times,
> We should respond in gratitude to the universal vow of great
> compassion.

791b

Respectfully.

Bunmei 7 (1475), 2.25

9. On the Anniversary of Master Shinran's Death

Today being the [monthly] anniversary of Master [Shin]ran's death, there are few people who do not intend by all means to repay their indebtedness and express their gratitude for his benevolence. What everyone must understand, however, is how difficult it will be for people to conform to the intention of our Master if (as in the case of practitioners who have not attained true and real faith through the power of the Primal Vow and in whom the settled mind is yet to be realized [*mianjin*]) they make the visit perfunctorily, for today only, and think that what is essential in the Shinshū is just filling the members' meeting place. Nevertheless, it is probably good for those who are not concerned about the thanksgiving services to be here, even if they attend reluctantly.

Those who intend to come without fail on the twenty-eighth of every month [must understand that] people in whom the settled mind is yet to be realized (*mianjin*) and for whom the customary ways of faith are not decisively established should, by all means, quickly attain other-power faith based on the truth and reality of the Primal Vow, thereby decisively settling the birth that is to come in the fulfilled land. It is this that will truly accomplish their [own] resolve to repay their indebtedness and express their gratitude for the

Master's benevolence. This also means that, as a matter of course, their objective of birth in the Land of Utmost Bliss is assured. It is, in other words, entirely consistent with what is expressed in [Shandao's] commentary (*Ōjō raisange,* T.47:442a):

> To realize faith oneself and to guide others to faith is the most difficult of all difficulties; to tell of great compassion and awaken beings everywhere is truly to respond in gratitude to the Buddha's benevolence.

Although more than a hundred years have already passed since the Master's death, we gratefully revere the image before our eyes. And although his benevolent voice is distant, separated from us by the wind of impermanence, his words of truth have been directly transmitted by his descendents; they resound with clarity deep in our ears. Thus it is that our school's faith, grounded in the truth and reality of other-power, has been transmitted until today without interruption. 791c

Therefore, given this present occasion, if there are people who have not realized the faith that is the truth and reality of the Primal Vow, we must indeed conclude they have not received the prompting of good from the past. If there were not people for whom good from the past had unfolded, all would be in vain and the birth that is to come [in the Pure Land] could not be settled. This would be the one thing to be lamented above all else.

And yet, although it is now difficult to encounter the one way of the Primal Vow, we are, on occasions, able to meet this supreme Primal Vow. This is indeed the joy of all joys—what could compare with it? We should revere [the Primal Vow]; we should entrust ourselves to it. People who thus overturn the evil delusions that have persisted in their minds over time and are then and there grounded in other-power faith, based on the ultimate truth of the Primal Vow, will truly conform to the Master's intention. This in itself will surely fulfill our resolve to repay our indebtedness and express our gratitude for the Master's benevolence today.

Respectfully.
Written on the twenty-eighth day
of the fifth month, Bunmei 7 (1475).

10. On Six Items, Including
"*Kami* Manifestations"

Followers of our tradition should be aware of the significance of the provisions of the six items [below] and, inwardly entrusting themselves deeply to the buddha-dharma, should act in such a way as to give no outward sign of it.

Therefore, it is a serious error that, these days, nenbutsu people in our tradition deliberately make known to those of other sects the way things are in our school. To put it briefly: from now on you must follow the buddha-dharma, observing the intent of these provisions. Those who go against these rules will no longer be counted among the followers [of our tradition].

> *Item:* Do not make light of [Shintō] shrines.
> *Item:* Do not make light of the buddhas, bodhisattvas, or [Buddhist] temples [enshrining deities].
> *Item:* Do not slander other sects or other teachings.
> *Item:* Do not slight the provincial military governors or local land stewards.
> *Item:* The interpretation of the buddha-dharma in this province is wrong; therefore, turn to the right teaching.
> *Item:* other-power faith as established in our tradition must be decisively settled deep in our hearts and minds.

First, all "*kami* manifestations" are transformations; in their original state, they are buddhas and bodhisattvas, but when they look upon the sentient beings of this realm, they realize that it is somewhat difficult [for those beings] to approach buddhas and bodhisattvas. Hence they appear provisionally as *kami* as a compassionate means of forming a bond with sentient beings and of encouraging them, through the strength [of that bond], to enter finally into the buddha-dharma. This is the meaning of [the passage] that says (*Makashikan,* T.46:80a):

> The first stage in forming a bond is softening the light and mixing with the dust; the final stage in benefiting beings is [manifesting] the eight aspects and attaining the way.

Therefore sentient beings in the present world [should realize that] those who entrust themselves to the buddha-dharma and say the nenbutsu will

surely be recognized by *kami* [in their various] manifestations as [the fulfillment of] their original intent. For this reason, although we do not specifically   792b
worship *kami* or entrust ourselves to them, when we take refuge in the compassionate vow of the one Amida Buddha, the thought of similarly entrusting
ourselves to [the *kami*] is encompassed within that.

Second, as buddhas and bodhisattvas are the original state for *kami* manifestations, when sentient beings of the present time entrust themselves to
Amida Tathāgata and say the nenbutsu, the other buddhas and bodhisattvas
feel that this is the fulfillment of their original intent, since they all rely on
their original teacher, Amida Tathāgata. For this reason, although we do not
rely specifically on the other buddhas, when we entrust ourselves to the one
buddha, Amida Buddha, all the buddhas and bodhisattvas are encompassed—
each and every one. Simply realize that when we take refuge in Amida Tathāgata singleheartedly and steadfastly, all the other buddhas' wisdom and virtue
come to be encompassed within one body, Amida [and so become ours].

Third, it is a great mistake to slander other sects and other teachings. The
reason for this was shown long ago in the three Pure Land sutras. Moreover,
scholars of other sects should never disparage people of the nenbutsu. In
view of the law [of karma], it is clear that neither [followers of] our sect nor
[those of] others can escape retribution for this offense.

Fourth, in regard to the provincial military governors and local land stewards, deal carefully with fixed yearly tributes and payments to officials and,
besides that, take [the principles of] humanity and justice as fundamental.

Fifth, the interpretation of the buddha-dharma in this province is not the
right teaching of our tradition; it appears to be a wrong view. In brief: listening
from now on to our tradition's right teaching, which is true and real, you must
overturn customary evil attachments and move toward a mind that is good.

Sixth, true people of the nenbutsu in our tradition fully know the right   792c
teaching established by the founder and, although they commit evil and lack
good, they take attainment of birth in the Land of Utmost Bliss to be the fundamental intent of our sect.

The right understanding of our school's settled mind is that, without any
striving, we rely singleheartedly and steadfastly on Amida Tathāgata and recognize how inconceivable it is that, although we are wretched beings burdened
with evil deeds and blind passion, the working of Amida's Vow—the strong

cause [of birth]—is directed toward saving such worthless beings; and when just a single thought free of doubt becomes firm, Amida unfailingly sends forth his unhindered light and embraces us. People who have undergone a decisive settling of faith in this way will all, each and every one, be born in the fulfilled land—ten people out of ten. What this means, in other words, is that these are people in whom other-power faith is decisively settled.

Above and beyond this, what we should bear in mind is that it is indeed [through] Amida Tathāgata's gracious and vast benevolence [that birth in the Pure Land is settled]; and with this realization, sleeping or waking, we simply say *Namu-amida-butsu* in gratitude for the Buddha's benevolence. What else, then, do we need besides this for [birth in] the afterlife? Is it not truly deplorable that [some people] confuse others by talking about false teachings that are of uncertain origin and are unknown to us, and furthermore that they debase the transmission of the Dharma? You must reflect on this very carefully.

Respectfully.

Bunmei 7 (1475), 7.15

11. On the Services Held Every Year without Exception

793a   As the twenty-eighth of this month is the anniversary [of the death] of our founder, Master [Shinran], services [have been held] every year without exception, in recognition of our indebtedness and in grateful response to [his] benevolence. Even the most humble fellow practitioners [come at this time] from the various provinces and districts; those who fail to recognize their indebtedness must indeed be like wood and stones!

Although this foolish old man has somehow lived for the past four or five years in the Hokuriku, in a remote corner of the mountains by the sea, it is beyond all expectation that he is still alive and has come to this province, and that this year, for the first time, we shall celebrate thanksgiving services together [in honor] of the Master's anniversary. This is indeed the [result of] inconceivable past conditions; I rejoice over it more and more deeply, time and again.

People who gather from this and other provinces should, therefore, first of all, be fully aware of the significance of the regulations established by the

94

founding Master. He said, "Even if you are called a 'cow thief,' do not act in such a way that you are seen as a follower of the buddha-dharma or as an aspirant for [buddhahood in] the afterlife." Besides this, he also carefully stipulated that we should observe [the principles of] humanity, justice, propriety, wisdom, and sincerity; that we should honor the laws of the state; and that, deep within, we should take other-power faith, established by the Primal Vow, as fundamental.

But recently, although people these days act as if they knew the buddha-dharma, [it is clear] from what I have observed that while they give an outward appearance of relying on the buddha-dharma, there is no decisive settling of faith (*anjin*), the single path in our tradition. Besides that, on the strength of their own ability, they read texts that are not authenticated in our tradition and then talk about unknown, false teachings. Wandering among the followers of our [sect] and others, they make up lies and, finally, under "orders from the head temple," they deceive people and take things [from them], thereby debasing the fundamental principles of our tradition. Is this not truly deplorable? 793b

Therefore, unless each of these people repents and confesses his evil ways and turns to the right teaching during the seven-day thanksgiving services [commemorating] the anniversary of the Master's death on the twenty-eighth of this month, [their coming will be to no purpose]; and if they attend these seven-day thanksgiving services just in imitation of others, though they say that they come to repay their indebtedness and express their gratitude for the [Master's] benevolence, [their coming] will amount to nothing at all. Hence it is precisely those people who have attained faith through the working of Amida's Vow who will return the Buddha's benevolence in gratitude and respond gratefully to their teacher's virtue. Those who thoroughly understand this and come to pay homage to the Master are the ones who are truly in accord with [Amida's] intention; they, in particular, will be deeply possessed of the resolve to repay their indebtedness and express their gratitude for his benevolence during this month's anniversary.

Respectfully.
Written on the twenty-first day
of the eleventh month, Bunmei 7 (1475).

12. On the Presence or Absence
of Good from the Past

These days, as in the past, it seems that many of those who call themselves followers of the buddha-dharma and extol and proclaim the teaching in various places in the provinces are themselves not truly grounded in the right teaching of our tradition. When we ask the reason for this, [the answer is that] in the first place, although they act as if they knew the buddha-dharma in depth, no part of their understanding has been gained from authentic sources. Some have heard the teaching quite by chance, from the edge of a veranda or from outside a sliding door; their aspiration for the buddha-dharma is in truth shallow, and they think there is no one who knows better than they what the buddha-dharma is all about. Consequently, when they happen to see people who proclaim our tradition's right teaching in the correct manner, they cling persistently to their own biased views. Is it not, in the first place, arrogance for them to assume immediately that only they fully know [the teaching]?

In this frame of mind, they wander from place to place among followers [of our tradition] and read the scriptures and, in addition to that, they simply ingratiate themselves with people, make up lies, and take things [from them], saying that they are sent from the main temple when they are carrying out personal matters. How can these people be called good followers of the buddha-dharma or readers of scripture? This is utterly deplorable. It is the one thing we should lament above all else. Those who want to present our tradition's teaching and instruct others must therefore, first of all, be fully aware of the steps in instruction.

When we consider presenting our tradition's other-power faith, we must first distinguish between the people who have good from the past and those who lack good from the past. For, however long ago a person may have listed his name as a participant in this [tradition], it will be difficult for one who lacks good from the past to attain faith. Indeed, faith (*shin*) will of itself be decisively settled in the person for whom past good has unfolded. And so, when we discuss the two [kinds of] practices—right and sundry—in the presence of people who lack good from the past, this may lay the foundation for slander, contrary to what one would expect. To teach extensively in the presence of ordinary people without understanding this principle of the presence

793c

794a

96

or absence of good from the past is in total opposition to our tradition's rules of conduct.

Hence the *Larger Sutra* says, "If a person lacks roots of good, he will not be able to hear this sutra" (*Daimuryōjukyō,* T.12:273a; *Kyōgyōshinshō,* T.83:630c) and "To hear this sutra and to sustain faith (*shingyō*) are the most difficult of all difficulties; nothing surpasses these difficulties" (*Daimuryō-jukyō,* T.12:279a; *Kyōgyōshinshō,* T.83:631c). Also, Shandao states: "If a person has already practiced this Dharma at one time in the past and is able to hear it again now, he will immediately realize joy" (*Kangyōsho,* T.37:264a).

In any case, it is clear, according to the sutras and commentaries, that everything depends on good from the past. Thus we understand that we should watch over people in whom there is good from the past and transmit the Dharma of our tradition to them. We must be fully aware of the significance of this and then instruct others.

In particular, first of all, take the laws of the state as fundamental and, giving priority to [the principles of] humanity and justice, follow the generally accepted customs; deep within yourself, maintain the settled mind of our tradition; and outwardly conduct yourself in such a way that the transmission of the Dharma you have received will not be evident to those of other sects and other schools. This distinguishes the person who fully knows our tradition's right teaching, which is true and real.

Respectfully.
Bunmei 8 (1476), 1.27

Shōnyo, disciple of Śākyamuni
(written seal)

13. On Followers of
Our Tradition

Followers of our tradition—both those in whom the settled mind is already established and those [whose faith is] yet to be established but who seek to attain the settled mind—must bear in mind the following points:

First of all, outwardly take the laws of the state as fundamental; do not hold any of the *kami,* buddhas, or bodhisattvas in contempt; do not slander

794b   other sects or other teachings. Do not slight the provincial military governors or local landowners, but meet fixed yearly tributes and payments to officials in full. Besides that, take [the principles of] humanity and justice as essential. Inwardly, rely singleheartedly and steadfastly on Amida Tathāgata for [birth in the Pure Land in] the afterlife and give no thought to any of the sundry practices and miscellaneous good acts; when we entrust ourselves without a single thought of doubt, we will be born without fail in the true and real Pure Land of Utmost Bliss. With this understanding, one is to be declared a nenbutsu follower who has realized faith through Amida Tathāgata's other-power.

    Having thus attained the faith that is expressed through the nenbutsu, we should then realize that, although we are wretched beings of deep evil karma who commit evil all our lives, when we once awaken faith with the one thought-moment of taking refuge [in Amida], we are readily saved by the working of the Buddha's Vow. Then, deeply recognizing the graciousness of Amida Tathā-gata's inconceivable, all-surpassing Primal Vow—the strong cause [of birth]—we simply say the nenbutsu, sleeping or waking, in gratitude for the Buddha's benevolence, and repay our indebtedness to Amida Tathāgata.

    Nothing we know beyond this is of any use for the [attainment of birth in the] afterlife, but these days, people talk absurdly—as if something were lacking—about unknown, eccentric teachings that have not been transmitted [within our tradition]; thus they confuse others and debase the unsurpassed

794c   transmission of the Dharma. This is indeed a deplorable situation. We must think about it very carefully.

Respectfully.

Bunmei 8 (1476), 7.18

Fascicle IV

1. On Shinshū Nenbutsu Practitioners

There are many among the Shinshū practitioners of the nenbutsu who have no understanding of the Dharma. Hence I have, for the most part, set down the main points. In brief, practitioners of the same mind are to take these words as fundamental from now on.

There are two points in regard to this. First, before all else, one must be settled in the faith (*anjin*) through which one's own birth [in the Pure Land] is accomplished. Second, in teaching others, one must determine the presence or absence of good from the past. We must keep these principles firmly in mind.

As for the first matter of one's own birth, store the faith that is awakened in the one thought-moment deeply within yourselves; moreover, persevere in saying the Name in gratitude for [Amida] Buddha's benevolence through other-power. In addition to this, honor the laws of the state and take [the principles of] humanity and justice as fundamental. Further, do not slight the various [*kami* and] buddhas and bodhisattvas, or belittle other teachings and other sects; simply follow the customs of ordinary life. Outwardly, do not show your devotion to our tradition to those of other sects and other schools. By this, one is to be declared a Shinshū nenbutsu practitioner who observes the regulations of our tradition's Master [Shinran]. In particular, act with extreme caution, as this is a time when people determinedly strain their ears to hear anything that can be distorted and spread in slander.

The "other-power threefold entrusting" taught in our tradition is described   795a
in the Eighteenth Vow [in the *Larger Sutra*] as "with sincere mind, entrusting and aspiring to be born in my land" (*Daimuryōjukyō*, T.12:268a; *Songō shinzō meimon*, T.83:679a). Although we call this "threefold entrusting," it is simply the one mind [of faith] in which a practitioner takes refuge, relying on Amida. That is to say, with the awakening of the one thought-moment in which a practitioner for whom past good has unfolded takes refuge in Amida, the Buddha embraces that practitioner (who has taken refuge through the one

99

thought-moment) with his compassionate light. Indicating this moment, we speak of "threefold entrusting—with sincere mind, entrusting and aspiring to be born." The passage on the fulfillment of the Vow [in the *Larger Sutra*] further explains it as "immediately attaining birth [in the Pure Land] and dwelling in [a state of] nonretrogression" (*Daimuryōjukyō,* T.12:272b; *Jōdo monrui jushō,* T.83:646b). Or again, we may say that [a person in] this state is a person of true and real faith, a practitioner with deep past causes, and one who has completed the cause [of birth] in ordinary life. Hence there is nothing, be it taking refuge in Amida or attaining faith, that is not related to good from the past.

We find, therefore, that if people who [seek] birth through the nenbutsu [do not realize faith] through the prompting of past causes, the birth to come in the fulfilled land is impossible. In the words of the Master, the point of this is: "If you should realize faith, rejoice in conditions from the distant past" (*Jōdo monrui jushō,* T.83:645a). And so, the understanding in our tradition is that efforts to teach others will be useless if we fail to determine the presence or absence of good from the past. For this reason, one should instruct others after having considered their innate capacity [for birth] in light of the existence or nonexistence of good from the past.

795b
Recently, the way of followers of the buddha-dharma in our tradition has been to talk indiscreetly about the teaching with no clear understanding of what is right and what is wrong. Hence we hear that the true meaning of Shin teaching has been utterly lost. It is with detailed knowledge of the above that one is to proclaim our tradition's basic principles.

Respectfully.
Bunmei 9 (1477), 1.8

2. On the Allotted Span of Life

If we calculate the length of human life, the allotted span at this time is fifty-six years. At present, however, it is indeed noteworthy for a person to have lived to be fifty-six. Given this, at sixty-three, I am already well into the years of decline. By my count, my life has already been extended by seven years. I feel uneasy on this point as to what sort of illness I may encounter in meeting the conditions leading to death, this being the working effect of karma from the past. This is something that certainly cannot be predicted.

In particular, as I observe the present state of affairs, [it is clear that] because this is a time of instability, human sorrow exceeds all imagination. If this is a world where we can surely die at once if we want to die, why have I lived on until now? Quite simply, the place where I am eager to be born is the Pure Land of utmost bliss, and what I aspire to and long to attain is the undefiled buddha body. But then, for a person who has, through the wisdom of the Buddha, realized the settled mind that is other-power [with the awakening] of the one thought-moment of taking refuge, what could be lacking that he would hasten the time of death established in a previous life (having reached the point of devoting himself until his life's end to the saying of the Name in grateful return for the Buddha's benevolence)? To the contrary, he might be foolishly deluded. Such is the reflection of this foolish old man. 795c Others, too, should be of this mind.

The way of the world is, above all, that we continue on as if unaware of the uncertainty of life for young and old alike. Existence is as ephemeral as a flash of lightning or the morning dew, and the wind of impermanence may come even now. Yet we think only of prolonging this life for as long as possible, without ever aspiring to [birth in the Pure Land] in the afterlife. This is inexpressibly deplorable.

From today, we should quickly entrust ourselves to Amida Tathāgata's Primal Vow of other-power. Steadfastly taking refuge in the Buddha of Immeasurable Life, we should aspire to birth in the true and real fulfilled land and repeat the nenbutsu, saying the Name of the Buddha.

Respectfully.

When [these thoughts] suddenly came to mind, I wrote them down quickly, finishing before seven in the morning, on the seventeenth day of the ninth month, Bunmei 9 (1477).

Shinshō-in [Rennyo]. Age 63.

Though written to be left behind,
This is a letter

101

That simply flowed from the brush—
Phrases here and there
May indeed seem strange.

3. On the Present Plight
of the World

The present plight of the world is such that no one knows when things will settle down. Consequently, as this is a time when it is difficult even to pass along the roads between the provinces, it is a period of utter confusion for the buddha-dharma and for mundane law. As a result, in some instances, no one even visits the temples and shrines of wondrous effects.

When we hear, in regard to this, that the human realm is [a place of] uncertainty for young and old alike, [we might feel that] we should quickly cultivate whatever meritorious good deeds may be possible and aspire to whatever enlightenment and nirvana may be attainable. Yet, at this time—though we call the present world "the last Dharma age of defilement and confusion"— Amida Tathāgata's other-power Primal Vow is mysteriously thriving all the more. Therefore, laypeople [must understand] that unless they rely on this vast, compassionate vow, realize the one thought-moment of faith, and attain birth in the Pure Land of suchness (eternity and bliss), it is indeed as if they went to a mountain of treasure and returned empty-handed. Quiet your minds and deeply reflect on this.

Thus it is that when we inquire in detail about the vows of all the buddhas, we hear that they were unable to save women burdened with the five obstacles and evildoers who had committed the five grave offenses. We are reminded in regard to this that it was Amida Tathāgata who alone made an unsurpassed, incomparable Vow—the great Vow that he would save ordinary beings burdened with evils and offenses and women burdened with the five obstacles. How gracious [a vow]—and how inadequate words are to describe it!

Accordingly, long ago, when Śākyamuni expounded the *Lotus* [*Sutra*], the wondrous text of the One Vehicle, on Mount Gṛdhrakūṭa, Devadatta provoked Ajātaśatru to acts of treachery; Śākya[muni] then led Vaidehī to aspire to the Land of Serene Sustenance. Because [Śākyamuni] withdrew from the assembly gathered at Mount Gṛdhrakūṭa where he was expounding the *Lotus* [*Sutra*], descended to the royal palace, and graciously set forth the Pure Land

796a

teaching for Vaidehī's sake, Amida's Primal Vow has flourished to this day. This is why we say that the teachings of the *Lotus Sutra* and the nenbutsu were given at the same time.

In other words, it is clear that Śākya[muni] used the five grave offenses in which Vaidehī, Devadatta, and Ajātaśatru were involved as compassionate means to cause women and those who have committed the five grave offenses in the last [Dharma] age to aspire to birth in the Land of Serene Sustenance; [he assured us that] even such people would unfailingly attain birth in the Land of Serene Sustenance if they took refuge in the inconceivable Primal Vow. This you should know.   796b

> Respectfully.
> Written on the twenty-seventh day
> of the ninth month, Bunmei 9 (1477).

4. On a Hymn in
Three Verses

As fall and spring slip away, the months and years go by; yesterday is spent, and today draws to a close. Little did I know that I would grow old before I was aware of it, with the unnoticed passage of the years. Yet, on occasion during that time, I must have known the beauty of flowers and birds, the wind, and the moon; I must also have met with the joy and sorrow of pleasure and pain. But now there is not even a single instance that I remember in particular. How sad it is to have grown gray with age, having done no more than pass nights and days to no purpose! But when I deeply reflect on the apparent soundness of my own existence, not yet having been called away by the relentless wind of impermanence, it seems like a dream, like an illusion. As for now, there is nothing left but to aspire to the one way of getting out of birth and death. And so, when I hear that it is Amida Tathāgata's Primal Vow that readily saves sentient beings like ourselves in this evil future age, I feel truly confident and thankful.

When we simply take refuge in this Primal Vow with sincere mind, with the [awakening of the] one thought-moment in which there is no doubt, then, without any anxiety, birth [in the Pure Land] is assured if we die at that time. Or, if life is prolonged, then during that time, we should say the nenbutsu in

796c gratitude for the Buddha's benevolence and await our lives' end. As I have indeed heard that this is precisely what is meant by "completing the cause [of birth] in ordinary life," this teaching of decisively settled faith continues to sound in the depths of my ears even now. How grateful I am—and how inadequate it is to say only that!

And so, in overwhelming awe and thankfulness for Amida Tathāgata's Primal Vow of other-power, I shall express what is written above as a hymn, [simply] giving way to what rises to my lips:

> The mind
> That even once
> Relies on Amida: that mind
> Is in accord
> With the true Dharma.

> When, deeply burdened with evil karma,
> We come to rely profoundly
> On the Tathāgata,
> By the power of the Dharma,
> We will go to the West.

> When our minds
> Are settled in the path
> Of hearing the Dharma,
> Let us simply say
> *Namu-amida-butsu.*

I write this in spite of myself, in response to the incomparable single teaching of the Primal Vow. The meaning of the three verses is as follows:

The first tells what it is for faith to be decisively settled through the one thought-moment of taking refuge. The next verse gives the meaning of "unfailingly attaining nirvana," the benefit of "entering the company of those [whose birth is] truly settled." The intent of the next is to explain what it is to "know Amida's benevolence and express gratitude," once we have rejoiced in diamondlike faith.

I felt, then, that even such a quiet voicing as this, since it is based on the awakening of other-power faith, might at least serve as an act of devotion in

104

grateful return for Amida Buddha's benevolence. I also thought that those who hear, if they have [the necessary] past conditions, might come to the same mind. I am, however, already in my seventh decade and feel it ridiculous, particularly as one who is both foolish and untalented, to speak of the teaching in this inadequate and uninformed way; yet at the same time—simply filled with awe at the single path of the Primal Vow—I have written down these poor verses, letting them flow from the brush without further reflection. Let those who see them in days to come not speak badly of them. Indeed, they may serve as a condition leading to praise of the Buddha's teaching and as a cause leading to the turning of the Dharma wheel. By all means, let there never be any disparagement of them.

797a

Respectfully.

I have written this down in a short time by the fire, in the middle of the twelfth month, the ninth year of Bunmei.

The above letter was picked up in the road and brought back to this temple by [a priest of] Busshōji who was out on an errand and walking from Hari-no-kihara to Kuken-zaike.

Bunmei 9 (1477), 12.2

5. From the Middle Period
until the Present

Among those who have carried out the teaching of our tradition from the middle period [from the time of Kakunyo] until the present, some have done so without knowing at all whether [their listeners] have, or lack, good from the past. Simply put, you must be aware of this from now on. When you read the scriptures, for example, or when you speak [even] briefly about the teach-ing, you must [first] ascertain this, and then proclaim the Dharma as taught within our school; or, again, when people gather in large numbers to listen to the buddha-dharma and you feel that there may be some among those people who lack good from the past, you should not discuss the meaning of our school's true and real Dharma. Recently, however, as I observe how people preach, [it is clear that some] lack this awareness and simply feel that,

797b

whichever type of person the listener may be, he will surely be grounded in our tradition's faith (*anjin*) if they preach well. You should know that this is an error. Carry out the teaching of our tradition with full awareness of what is written above. From the middle period until now, there has been no one at all who has understood this and preached with excellence. You are to undertake preaching in the traditional way, fully recognizing these points. As the twenty-eighth of this month marks an annual ceremony, there are many who faithfully anticipate observing nenbutsu services to repay their indebtedness and express their gratitude for the benevolence of our founder, Master [Shinran]. This is because of their clearly knowing the truth of "drawing from the stream to discover the source" (*Hōonkō shiki,* T.83:756a). It is entirely due to the pervasiveness of the Master's teaching.

Meanwhile, in recent years, [some] have confused people to the extreme by spreading distorted teachings not discussed in our tradition. Others, reprimanded by local land stewards and domain holders, (who are themselves entrenched in wrong views,) have come to view our tradition's true and real faith (*anjin*) as mistaken. Is this not a deplorable situation? It is lamentable; it is dreadful.

In sum, during the seven days and nights of the thanksgiving services this month, each person should deeply repent; and, leaving none of his own mistaken thoughts at the bottom of his mind, he should undergo a turning of that mind and confess before the revered image [of the founder] in this temple, telling of this every day and every night so that everyone will hear about it. This, in other words, is in accord with [a passage in Shandao's] commentary (*Hōjisan,* T.47:426a; *Kyōgyōshinshō,* T.83:615c):

797c

> With a turning of the mind, [even] slanderers of the Dharma and those who lack the seed of buddhahood (*icchantika*) will all be born [in the Pure Land].

It also corresponds to the teaching of "realizing faith (*shin*) oneself and guiding others to faith (*shin*)." Then, on hearing about this turning of the mind and repentance, attentive people will indeed feel the rightness of it, and in some of them the ordinary "bad" mind may be similarly overturned and changed into the "good" mind. This will truly accomplish the fundamental purpose of the Master's anniversary this month. In other words, this is the offering through which we repay our indebtedness and express our gratitude [for his benevolence].

Respectfully.
Bunmei 14 (1482), 11.21

6. On Three Items

The thanksgiving services this month are held as an annual ceremony of long standing, marking the anniversary of the death of the founder, Master [Shinran]. Consequently, followers of our tradition in provinces far and near are filled with eagerness for the pilgrimage and wish to express the sincerity of their gratitude on this occasion. And so it is that, for seven days and nights every year, they concentrate on and devote themselves to nenbutsu services. This is precisely why practitioners of true and real faith are flourishing. Indeed, we might almost say that the period of firm practice of the nenbutsu has come.

Among those who make pilgrimages during the seven-day period as a result of this, there may indeed be some who come to worship before the revered image [of the founder] only in imitation of others. These people should promptly kneel before the revered image and, through a turning of the mind and repentance, enter into the true purport of the Primal Vow and attain true and real faith with the awakening of the one thought-moment [of entrusting].

798a

We must realize that *namu-amida-butsu* is the essence of the settled mind for nenbutsu practitioners. This is because *namu* means "to take refuge." We must know that, for ordinary beings like ourselves who lack good and do evil, "taking refuge" expresses the [entrusting] mind that relies on Amida Buddha. This entrusting mind is none other than the mind of Amida Buddha, who receives sentient beings into his great light of eighty-four thousand rays and grants to sentient beings the two aspects of the Buddha's directing of virtue, outgoing [from birth and death] and returning [into birth and death]. Thus faith has no other meaning than this. Everything is encompassed within *namu-amida-butsu.* Recently, some people have been thinking otherwise.

In regard to this, among the followers of our tradition in various provinces, there are many who confuse the meaning of the Dharma by propounding obscure teachings not prescribed in the scriptures designated by our founder. This is indeed ridiculous. In brief, people like these should certainly take part in this seven-day period of thanksgiving services, reverse their mistakes, and ground themselves in the right teaching.

Item: Those who are pillars of the buddha-dharma and hold the position of priest in accord with the tradition are said to have told others about false teachings that are unknown to us and of obscure origin and, recently, to have actively engaged in this far and wide in order to be considered learned. This is preposterous.

Item: It is a great mistake for people to announce that they are making a pilgrimage to the revered image [of the founder] at the Honganji, in Kyoto, and then to speak indiscriminately to others about matters concerning the buddha-dharma regardless of the sort of people who are around, especially on main roads and thoroughfares and at checking stations and ferry crossings.

Item: Should there be a situation in which someone asks what sort of buddha-dharma you rely on, do not answer outright that you are a nenbutsu person in our tradition. Simply reply that you are a person of no particular sect who just knows the nenbutsu to be something precious. This, in other words, is the bearing of a person who, as our tradition's Master taught, will not be seen as a follower of the buddha-dharma.

798b

You must recognize, therefore, that right understanding in our tradition is knowing these points thoroughly and giving no sign of them outwardly. Furthermore, none of the points established by the community during the thanksgiving services over the past two or three years are to be altered. If by chance there are points with which members of this community are at variance, those who differ can no longer be followers of the founding Master.

Respectfully.

Bunmei 15 (1483), 11

7. On Six Items

As the thanksgiving services this month are an annual ceremony of long standing, there has been no lapse up to now in our seven-day observations of them.

On this occasion, therefore, followers from various provinces come with an   798c
earnest resolve to repay their indebtedness and express their gratitude; they
devote themselves to the fundamental practice of the nenbutsu, saying the
Name of the Buddha. This is indeed the virtue of the single practice and the
singlemindedness through which birth [in the Pure Land] is settled.

In regard to those on pilgrimage from the provinces, however, it seems
that few dwell in the same faith (*anjin*). The reason for this is that their aspiration is not truly for the buddha-dharma—and if they are simply imitating
others or following social convention, it is indeed a lamentable situation. For
when those in whom the settled mind is yet to be realized (*mianjin*) do not
even discuss their doubts, they betray the utmost lack of faith (*fushin*). And
so, although they endure a journey of thousands of *ri* and undergo great hardship in coming to the capital, it is to no purpose at all. This is utterly deplorable.
But if they are people lacking good from the past, perhaps we must say that
it cannot be helped.

> *Item:* Although it seems that the buddha-dharma has been flourishing
> in recent years, we hear that those who hold the position of priest are
> indeed the last ones to hold any discussion whatsoever of faith. This is
> a deeply lamentable situation.

> *Item:* There are many humble followers who hear the truth of other-
> power faith [without seeking instruction through the temples], and it is
> said that priests have been angry about this. This is preposterous.

> *Item:* There is a point to be borne in mind by each of those who come
> on pilgrimage from the countryside: it is inexcusable for them to discuss
> the buddha-dharma with no hesitation about being among outsiders or
> being on main roads and byways, at checking stations and on ferry boats.   799a
> This must definitely stop.

> *Item:* If there is a situation in which someone asks a nenbutsu person in
> our tradition what sect [he belongs to], he should not answer outright
> that he is a nenbutsu person of this sect. He should simply reply that he
> is a nenbutsu person of no particular sect. This, in other words, is the
> conduct [of one] who, as our Master taught, will not be seen as a follower
> of the buddha-dharma. Be thoroughly aware of this point and give no

outward sign [of being a participant in our tradition]. This indeed is the right understanding in regard to the conduct of nenbutsu people in our tradition.

Item: Even if you feel that you understand the significance of the buddha-dharma—having listened through sliding doors or over a hedge—faith will be decisively settled [only] by your repeatedly and carefully asking others about its meaning. If you leave things to your own way of thinking, there will invariably be mistakes. It has been said recently that there are such instances these days.

Item: You should ask others, time after time, about what you have understood of faith until other-power faith (*anjin*) is decisively settled. If you listen but once, there will surely be mistakes.

The above six items should be carefully borne in mind. I have noticed recently that, although everyone listens to the buddha-dharma, there is no one who has undergone a true and real settling of faith by just hearing the teaching in a general way; consequently, [their realization of] the settled mind, too, is not as it should be.

799b

Respectfully.

Bunmei 16 (1484), 11.21

8. On Eight Items

The thanksgiving services on the twenty-eighth of this month are a tradition handed down from the past. Accordingly, this is the occasion on which followers from provinces far and near come with an earnest resolve to repay their indebtedness and express their gratitude [for the benevolence of Master Shinran]. There has been no lapse these days or in the past in the continual repetition of the nenbutsu, the saying of the Buddha's Name. This is the legacy of the founding Master's transmission of the Dharma, the peerless teaching that extends to all under heaven and across the four seas.

On this occasion of seven days and nights, therefore, let those persons who oppose the Dharma in their lack of faith (*fushin*) attain the faith that leads to birth in the Pure Land. This in itself would serve as a repayment of indebtedness on the Master's anniversary this month. It may be that those who fail to do so are lacking in resolve to repay their indebtedness and express their gratitude. For, among those who call themselves Shinshū nenbutsu people, there are some these days who have not truly—from the bottom of their hearts—undergone a decisive settling of our tradition's faith (*anjin*); some give every indication of expressing gratitude for [the sake of] reputation, others perfunctorily. This is a situation that should never be. For it is a lamentable state of affairs that those who come to the capital, having endured a journey of thousands of *ri* and undergone great hardship, should then be uselessly concerned with reputation or blindly follow others. It must be emphasized that this is extremely shallow thinking. But for those lacking good from the past, it cannot be helped. If they make a full confession, however, and direct themselves toward the right-mindedness of the one mind [of faith], they may yet achieve the Master's fundamental intent.

> *Item:* Among those on pilgrimage from the various provinces, there are 799c some who, regardless of where they are—even on main roads and thoroughfares, at checking stations and on ferry boats—talk to others openly about matters concerning the buddha-dharma. This should not be.
>
> *Item:* In various places, there are many who praise [obscure,] rarely encountered teachings that we do not discuss at all in our tradition; similarly, they use strange phrases not found in our sect's teachings. This is seriously mistaken thinking. From now on, it must definitely stop.
>
> *Item:* During this seven-day period of thanksgiving services, those whose faith is not settled should, without exception, make up their minds to repent and confess without holding back anything in their hearts and then attain true and real faith.
>
> *Item:* There are some people who have not yet undergone any decisive settling of faith (*anjin*) and should for this reason raise their doubts. However, they keep these things to themselves and do not talk openly about them. When we press and question them, they just try to evade the point, without saying frankly what is on their minds. This is inexcusable. They should speak unreservedly and thus ground themselves in true and real faith.

111

Item: In recent years, priests who are pillars of the buddha-dharma have been seriously lacking in faith while followers [of the tradition], companions, have, on the contrary, undergone a decisive settling of faith. When they then talk about the priests' lack of faith, [the priests] become very angry. This is absurd. From now on, both priests and disciples must abide in the same faith.

Item: Recently, there have been rumors of extremely heavy drinking on the part of those in the position of priest. This is outrageous; such a thing should not be. We do not tell those who drink intoxicants that they must stop altogether. [But] when there is heavy drinking, there are sure to be times when there is nothing but drunken confusion in connection with the buddha-dharma and with followers; thus it is improper. If those in the priest's position stop on such occasions, they will indeed contribute to the prospering of the buddha-dharma. If they are unable to stop completely, one cup may be permissible. It may follow as a matter of course that they do not stop because their aspiration in regard to the buddha-dharma is weak. These are points that deserve deep reflection.

Item: If those in whom faith is decisively settled have frequent discussions of faith with each other when there are meetings for fellow practitioners, this will provide the basis on which the Shinshū will flourish.

Item: It must be understood that the decisive settling of faith in our tradition is expressed by the six characters *na-mu-a-mi-da-butsu.* Shandao explained long ago in his commentary: "*Namu* means 'to take refuge.' It also signifies aspiring to be born and directing virtue. *Amida-butsu* is the practice" (*Kangyōsho,* T.37:250ab; *Kyōgyōshinshō,* T.83:594c).

When sentient beings take refuge in Amida [saying] *namu,* Amida Buddha, fully knowing those sentient beings, bestows on them the virtue of a myriad of good deeds and practices, countless as the grains of sand in the Ganges River. This is what is meant by "*Amida-butsu* is the practice." Those who take refuge (*namu*) are therefore one with the saving Dharma of Amida Buddha; we speak of "the oneness in *namu-amida-butsu* of the person [to be saved] and the Dharma [that saves]," indicating this point. We must bear in mind, therefore, that *namu-amida-butsu*

800a

800b

112

expresses the full realization of perfect enlightenment [that was accomplished] when Amida Buddha vowed long ago when he was the *bhikṣu* Dharmākara that unless sentient beings attained buddhahood, he too would not attain perfect enlightenment. This, in other words, is evidence that our birth [in the Pure Land] is settled. Hence it should be concluded that our realization of other-power faith is expressed in just these six characters.

The significance of these eight items is as stated. Meanwhile, it has already been nine years since [we began] the construction of this temple. During the thanksgiving services each year, everyone feels that he has fully heard and understood [the teaching] and undergone a decisive settling of faith; but as the meaning of that faith differs even as of yesterday and today, it may amount to nothing at all. But if those lacking faith (*fushinjin*) do not quickly attain true and real faith during the thanksgiving services this month—during this year's thanksgiving services in particular—it seems things will be the same, even with the passage of many years.

This foolish old man has, however, already passed his seventh decade and finds it difficult to anticipate next year's thanksgiving services. For this reason, if there are people who really and truly attain decisively settled faith (*shin*), I would consider [their realization] to be, first, an expression of gratitude to the Master this month, and, next, the fulfillment of a desire an old man has cherished over these seven or eight years.

Respectfully.
Bunmei 17 (1485), 11.23

9. On an Epidemic

Recently, people have been dying in great numbers, reportedly from an epidemic. It is not that they die primarily because of the epidemic. It is [because of] determinate karma that has been settled from the first moment of our births. We should not be so deeply surprised by this. And yet when people die at this time, everyone thinks it strange. It is really quite reasonable.

Amida Tathāgata has declared that he will unfailingly save those sentient beings who singleheartedly rely on him—ordinary beings in the last [Dharma] age and people like ourselves, burdened with evil karma, however deep the

800c

113

evil may be. At such a time as this, we should entrust ourselves to Amida Buddha all the more deeply and, realizing that we will be born in the Land of Utmost Bliss, relinquish every bit of doubt, steadfastly and singleheartedly acknowledging how gracious Amida is. Once we have understood this, our saying *Namu-amida-butsu, Namu-amida-butsu*—sleeping or waking—is an expression of gratitude conveying our joy and thankfulness [that Amida] really saves us in this way. This, in other words, is the nenbutsu of gratitude for the Buddha's benevolence.

Respectfully.

Entoku 4 (1492), 6

10. On the Present Age

Let all women living in the present age deeply entrust themselves with single-ness of mind to Amida Tathāgata. Apart from that, they must realize, they will never be saved in [regard to] the afterlife, whatever teaching they may rely upon.

801a

How, then, should they entrust themselves to Amida, and how should they aspire to the afterlife?

They should have no doubt at all that there will unfailingly be deliverance for those who, without any worry, simply rely singleheartedly on Amida and entrust themselves [to him] to save them, [bringing them to buddhahood] in the afterlife. Once [they have understood] this, they should just say the nenbutsu in gratitude for the Buddha's benevolence, recognizing it as [an expression of] thankfulness [for the fact] that there will assuredly be deliverance.

Respectfully.

Age 83. (seal)

11. On the Oneness of the Person [to Be Saved] and the Dharma [That Saves]

What is the meaning of *namu-amida-butsu*? And further, how are we to entrust ourselves to Amida and attain birth in the fulfilled land?

114

What we must understand, first of all, is that we entrust ourselves to Amida by carefully discerning what the six characters *na-mu-a-mi-da-butsu* are all about. *Namu-amida-butsu* is essentially nothing other than the [entrusting] mind of we sentient beings who rely on Amida to save us, [bringing us to buddhahood] in the afterlife. In other words, Amida Tathāgata, fully knowing the sentient beings who entrust themselves, readily bestows virtue of unsurpassed, great benefit. This is what is meant by saying that he "directs virtue to sentient beings." Therefore, because those who entrust themselves to Amida are inseparable from Amida Buddha's saving Dharma, we speak of this as "the oneness in *namu-amida-butsu* of the person [to be saved] and the Dharma [that saves]"; it has this meaning. We must bear in mind that this is other-power faith, through which our birth [in the Pure Land] is settled.

801b

The writing of this [letter] was completed on the twenty-fifth day of the fifth month, Meiō 6 (1497).

Age 83.

12. On Semimonthly Meetings

For what purpose have there come to be meetings twice each month? They are [held] for the sake of realizing one's own faith which leads to birth in the Land of Utmost Bliss and for nothing else. Although there have been "meetings" everywhere each month, from the past up until now, there has never been anything at all that might be called a discussion of faith. In recent years in particular, when there have been meetings (wherever they have been), everyone has dispersed after nothing more than sake, rice, and tea. This is indeed contrary to the fundamental intent of the buddha-dharma. Although each of those lacking faith (*fushin*) should by all means raise their doubts and discuss what it is to have faith or be without it, they take their leave without coming to any conclusions. This is not as it should be. You must carefully reflect on this matter. In brief, it is essential that each of those lacking faith (*fushin*) have discussions of faith with one another from now on.

The meaning of our tradition's settled mind is that, regardless of the depth of our own evil hindrances, there is no doubt whatsoever that [Amida] will save all sentient beings who simply put a stop to their inclination toward the sundry practices, singleheartedly take refuge in Amida Tathāgata, and deeply entrust themselves [to him] to save them in [regard to] the most important matter, [the birth] that is to come in the afterlife. Those who thoroughly understand in this way will indeed be born [in the Pure Land], one hundred out of one hundred.

801c   Once [they have understood] this, if they recognize the holding of meetings each month as a repayment of indebtedness and expression of gratitude, they may indeed be called practitioners endowed with true and real faith.

Respectfully.
Written on the twenty-fifth day
of the second month, Meiō 7 (1498).

To the members of the congregations that meet twice each month.

Age 84.

13. Reflections in Early Summer

Fall and spring have slipped away, and it is already the middle of early summer in this seventh year of Meiō; I have grown old—I am eighty-four. This particular year, however, I have been seriously beset by illness, and as a result my whole body has suffered—ears, eyes, hands, and feet. I realize, then, that this in itself is the outcome of past karma and also the harbinger of birth in the Land of Utmost Bliss. Master Hōnen said, pursuant to this, "Practitioners who aspire for the Pure Land are filled with joy when they become ill"; these are his very words. And yet, it never occurs to me to rejoice over illness. I am a shameful person. This is disgraceful; it is deplorable. Nevertheless, according to our sect's teaching of "completing the cause [of birth in the Pure Land] in ordinary life, with the awakening of the one thought-moment [of entrusting]," I am now settled in the single path of faith (*anjin*). [My] saying of the Name in grateful return for the Buddha's benevolence is therefore unceasing; walking, standing, sitting, or lying down, I am never forgetful.

What follows are the reflections of this foolish old man.

Generally speaking, in observing the attitude of followers of this sect in the various places where I have stayed, I have found no indication of faith being

802a   clearly and decisively settled. This is most lamentable. For if (in testimony to this old man having already lived some eighty years) there were a flourishing of practitioners for whom faith was decisively settled, this might be considered the mark of a long life. But I see no sign at all of [faith] being clearly settled.

What are the grounds [for this lament]? Considering that the human realm is a place of uncertainty for young and old alike, we will surely undergo some sort of illness and die. Everyone must understand that, given the circumstances in a world like this, it is essential that faith be settled decisively and promptly—indeed, as soon as possible—and that we be assured of the birth to come in the Land of Utmost Bliss. [It is also essential] that we live out our lives after that in conformity with the ordinary circumstances of human life. We must think seriously about this and, deep within, awaken the aspiration to entrust ourselves singlemindedly to Amida.

Respectfully.

Meiō 7 (1498), the first day of the middle period of early summer. Written by an old priest, eighty-four years of age.

> If ever we are able to hear
> The Name of Amida,
> Let us all entrust ourselves,
> *Namu-amida-butsu.*

14. On Our School's
Settled Mind

anjin

Our school's <u>settled mind</u> is expressed by the six characters *na-mu-a-mi-da-butsu*. This you should know. Master Shandao explains these six characters, saying (*Kangyōsho,* T.37:250ab; *Kyōgyōshinshō,* T.83:594c):

> *Namu* means "to take refuge." It also signifies aspiring to be born and directing virtue. *Amida-butsu* is the practice. Because of this, we unfailingly attain birth.

First, the two characters *na-mu* mean "to take refuge." "To take refuge" expresses the [entrusting] mind of sentient beings who rely on Amida Buddha to save them, [bringing them to buddhahood] in the afterlife. Then, "Aspiring for birth and directing virtue" expresses the [Buddha's] mind that embraces   802b and saves sentient beings who entrust themselves. This is the precise meaning of the four characters *a-mi-da-butsu.*

What attitude should ignorant sentient beings like ourselves take, then, and how should we entrust ourselves to Amida?

When we abandon the sundry practices and steadfastly and singleheartedly rely on Amida to save us in [regard to] the afterlife, there is no doubt at all that we will be born without fail in the Land of Utmost Bliss. Thus the two characters *na-mu* signify the sentient being, the person who relies on Amida. Further, the four characters *a-mi-da-butsu* express the Dharma that saves sentient beings who entrust themselves. This, then, is precisely what we mean by "the oneness in *namu-amida-butsu* of the person [to be saved] and the Dharma [that saves]." Through this teaching, we know that birth [in the Pure Land] for all of us sentient beings is realized in *namu-amida-butsu.*

Respectfully.

Meiō 7 (1498), 4

15. On Building [the Priest's Quarters] at Ōsaka

After seeing Ōsaka (in Ikutama estate, Higashinari district, Settsu province) for the first time, I had a simple temple built promptly in the traditional way, surely through some sort of link to the place from the past. [Building] began in the latter part of autumn in the fifth year of Meiō; as of this year, three years have already sped by. I feel this to be none other than the result of inconceivable conditions from the distant past.

802c My fundamental reason for being in this place, then, has never been to live out my life in tranquility, to seek wealth and fame, or to enjoy the beauty to be found in flowers and birds, the wind, and the moon; my only longing is that practitioners of decisively settled faith may flourish and that fellow practitioners who say the nenbutsu may come forth for the sake of supreme enlightenment (*bodhi*). Moreover, if there are any in the world who harbor prejudice [against us] or if any difficult issues arise, I will give up my attachment to this place and immediately withdraw. Therefore, if [everyone]— regardless of whether they are of noble or humble birth, priest or lay—could be brought to a definite settling of faith that is firm and diamondlike, this would truly be in accord with the Primal Vow of Amida Tathāgata and, in particular, in conformity with the fundamental intent of Master [Shinran].

It is extraordinary that, as of this year, this foolish old man has already lived to the age of eighty-four. And as this [life] may indeed have been in accord with the meaning of the Dharma in our tradition, I could know no greater satisfaction. But I have been ill since the summer of this year, and at present there is no sign of recovery. I feel it certain at last that I will not fail to attain my long-cherished desire of birth [in the Pure Land] during the coming winter. All I long for, morning and evening, is that there will be a decisive settling of faith for everyone while I am still alive. Although this does indeed depend on good from the past, there is never a moment when it is not on my mind. Moreover, it might even be considered the consequence of my having spent three years   803a in this place. By all means, then, let there be a decisive settling of faith during this seven-day period of thanksgiving services so that everyone may realize the fundamental intent [of the Dharma], birth in the Land of Utmost Bliss.

Respectfully.

This letter is to be read, beginning on the twenty-first day of the eleventh month of Meiō 7 (1498), so that everyone may receive faith (*shin*).

Shōnyo, disciple of Śākyamuni
(written seal)

Fascicle V

1. On Laymen and Laywomen Lacking Wisdom in the Last [Dharma] Age

Laymen and laywomen lacking wisdom in the last [Dharma] age [should realize that] sentient beings who rely deeply and with singleness of mind on Amida Buddha and entrust themselves singleheartedly and steadfastly (without ever turning their minds in any other direction) to the Buddha to save them are unfailingly saved by Amida Tathāgata, even if their evil karma is deep and heavy. This is the essence of the Eighteenth Vow of birth [in the Pure Land] through the nenbutsu.

Once [faith] has been decisively settled in this way, they should—sleeping or waking—repeat the nenbutsu, saying the Name of the Buddha as long as they live.

Respectfully.

2. On the Eighty Thousand Teachings

It has been said that those who do not know [the importance of] the afterlife are foolish, even though they may understand eighty thousand sutras and teachings; those who know about the afterlife are wise, even though they may be unlettered men and women who have renounced the world while remaining in lay life. The import of our tradition is, therefore, that for those who do not realize the significance of the one thought-moment of faith— even though they may diligently read the various scriptures and be widely informed—all is in vain. This you should know.

803b

Therefore, as the Master [Shinran] has said, no men or women will ever be saved without entrusting themselves to Amida's Primal Vow. Hence there should be no doubt at all that those who abandon the sundry practices and, with [the awakening of] the one thought-moment, deeply entrust themselves to Amida Tathāgata to save them in [regard to] the afterlife will all be born in Amida's fulfilled land, whether ten people or one hundred—whatever sort of [men or] women they may be.

Respectfully.

3. On Women Who Have Renounced the World while Remaining in Lay Life and on Ordinary Women

Women who have renounced the world while remaining in lay life and ordinary women as well should realize and have absolutely no doubt whatsoever that there is deliverance for all those who simply rely deeply (singleheartedly and steadfastly) on Amida Buddha and entrust themselves to [the Buddha] to save them, [bringing them to buddhahood] in the afterlife. This is the Primal Vow of other-power, the Vow of Amida Tathāgata. Once [they have realized] this, when they then feel thankfulness and joy at being saved in [regard to] the afterlife, they should simply repeat *Namu-amida-butsu, Namu-amida-butsu.*

Respectfully.

4. On Men and Women

Those of deep evil karma, both men and women, [should realize that] even if they entrust themselves to the compassionate vows of the various buddhas, it is extremely difficult for them [to be saved] by the power of those buddhas, since the present period is the evil world of the last [Dharma] age. Therefore, 803c the one we revere as Amida Tathāgata, surpassing all [other] buddhas, made the great Vow that he would save even evildoers who have committed the ten transgressions and the five grave offenses; [fulfilling the Vow], he became Amida Buddha. Since it is Amida who vowed that he would not attain enlightenment if he failed to save sentient beings who deeply rely on this buddha and singlemindedly entrust themselves [to him] to save them, there is no doubt at all that they will be born in the Land of Utmost Bliss.

Hence it is certain that those who, without doubting, deeply (singleheartedly and steadfastly) entrust themselves to Amida Tathāgata to save them, leave their deep evil karma to the Buddha, and undergo a settling of the one thought-moment of faith will all be born in the Pure Land—ten out of ten, one hundred out of one hundred. Once [they have realized] this, then when a sense of awe wells up in their hearts, they should say the nenbutsu, *Namu-amida-butsu, Namu-amida-butsu,* whatever the hour, wherever they may be. This, in other words, is the nenbutsu of gratitude for the Buddha's benevolence.

Respectfully.

5. On Realizing Faith

Realizing faith means understanding the Eighteenth Vow. Understanding this vow means understanding what *namu-amida-butsu* is. For within the one thought-moment of taking refuge—*namu*—there is aspiration for birth and directing of virtue. This, in other words, is the mind that Amida Tathāgata directs to ordinary beings. In the *Larger Sutra,* this is explained as "enabling all sentient beings to fulfill their virtue" (*Daimuryōjukyō,* T.12:269c). Thus it is taught that the evil karma and blind passions accumulated from the beginningless past are extinguished (with no traces remaining) by the inconceivable working of the Vow, and that we dwell in the company of those [whose birth in the Pure Land is] truly settled, in the stage of nonretrogression. This, then, is what we mean by "attaining nirvana without severing blind passions" (*Kyōgyōshinshō,* T.83:600a). This is a matter presented exclusively in our tradition; there should be no discussion of the above with those of other traditions. Bear this carefully in mind.

804a

Respectfully.

6. On the Great Benefit Bestowed with [the Awakening of] the One Thought-moment [of Faith]

In the *Hymns* [*on the Last Dharma Age*], Master [Shinran] states that virtue of unsurpassed and great benefit is bestowed on practitioners who, with [the awakening of] the one thought-moment, entrust themselves to Amida (*Shōzō-matsu wasan,* T.83:665c):

When sentient beings of this evil world of the five defilements entrust themselves to the selected Primal Vow, indescribable, inexplicable, and inconceivable virtue fills the existence of these practitioners.

In this hymn, "sentient beings of this evil world of the five defilements" refers to all of us, [including] women and evildoers. Therefore although we are such wretched beings who commit evil throughout our lives, there is no doubt at all that those who rely singleheartedly and steadfastly on Amida Tathāgata and entrust themselves to [the Buddha] to save them in [regard to] the afterlife will unfailingly be saved. Amida bestows "indescribable, inexplicable, and inconceivable great virtue" on those who entrust themselves in this way.

"Indescribable, inexplicable, and inconceivable virtue" means unlimited great virtue. Because this great virtue is directed to us sentient beings who singlemindedly entrust ourselves to Amida, karma-hindrances of the three periods, past, future, and present, are instantly extinguished, and we are established in the stage of those who are truly settled, or in the stage equal to perfect enlightenment. Again, this is expressed in the *Hymns* [*on the Last Dharma Age*] (*Shōzōmatsu wasan,* T.83:664bc, 665b):

804b

Entrust yourselves to the Primal Vow of Amida.
All those who entrust themselves to the Primal Vow will,
Through the benefit of being embraced and never abandoned,
Reach [the stage] equal to perfect enlightenment.

"Being embraced and never abandoned" also means that sentient beings who singlemindedly entrust themselves to Amida are received within the [Buddha's] light, and that, since the entrusting mind does not change, they will not be forsaken. Although there are various teachings besides this, there should never be any doubt that sentient beings who entrust themselves solely to Amida in the one thought-moment will, each and every one, be born in the fulfilled land.

Respectfully.

7. On the Five Obstacles and the Three Submissions

Because the bodily existence of women is defined by the five obstacles and the three submissions, they are burdened with deep evil karma exceeding that of men. For this reason, the buddhas of the ten directions can never, by their own power, bring any woman to buddhahood. Yet Amida Tathāgata, having made the great Vow that he himself would save women, delivers them. Without entrusting herself to this buddha, a woman is unable to become a buddha.

What attitude should [a woman] have, then, and how should she entrust herself to Amida Buddha and become a buddha?

By just entrusting herself solely to Amida Buddha (with no double-mindedness, with steadfastness, and with the single thought that [Amida] saves her in [regard to] the afterlife) [a woman] will readily become a buddha. If 804c this mind is free of the slightest doubt, she will unfailingly go to the Land of Utmost Bliss and become a splendid buddha.

Once [she understands] this, what she must then bear in mind is that, whenever she says the nenbutsu, she says [it] only to express her joy and thankfulness for the benevolence of Amida Tathāgata who readily saves such a wretched being as herself. Let [this] be understood.

Respectfully.

8. On the Meditation for Five *Kalpa*s

Both the Primal Vow following the meditation for five *kalpa*s and the practice of numberless, uncountable *kalpa*s are simply compassionate means to save all of us sentient beings without fail. To this end, Amida Tathāgata underwent painstaking endeavors and made the Primal Vow, *namu-amida-butsu*; he became *namu-amida-butsu,* having vowed that he would not attain enlightenment if he failed to save sentient beings (erring beings) who, with [the awakening of] the one thought-moment, entrust themselves to Amida Buddha, abandon the sundry practices, and rely on Amida steadfastly and singleheartedly. We should know that this is precisely why it is that we are to be born readily in the Land of Utmost Bliss.

The meaning of the six characters *na-mu-a-mi-da-butsu* is, therefore, that all sentient beings are to be born in the fulfilled land. For when we take refuge—*namu*—Amida Buddha immediately saves us. Hence the two characters *na-mu* express sentient beings' turning to Amida Tathāgata and entrusting themselves [to Amida] to save them, [bringing them to buddhahood] in the afterlife. We must realize that those who entrust themselves to Amida in this way are saved without exception; this itself is the essence of the four characters *a-mi-da-butsu.*

805a

Therefore, those who abandon the sundry practices and wholeheartedly entrust themselves [to Amida] to save them in [regard to] the afterlife (even if they are women burdened with the ten transgressions and the five grave offenses, the five obstacles and the three submissions) will be saved without exception— each and every one, whether there are ten people or one hundred. Those who believe this without doubting will be born in Amida's true and real Pure Land.

Respectfully.

9. On All the Holy Texts

The meaning of settled mind in our tradition is wholly expressed by six characters, *na-mu-a-mi-da-butsu.* That is, when we take refuge—*namu*—Amida Buddha immediately saves us. Hence the two characters *na-mu* mean "taking refuge." "Taking refuge" signifies the mind of sentient beings who abandon the sundry practices and steadfastly entrust themselves to Amida Buddha to save them, [bringing them to buddhahood] in the afterlife. [The four characters *a-mi-da-butsu*] express the mind of Amida Tathāgata who, fully knowing sentient beings, saves them without exception.

Accordingly, since Amida Buddha saves sentient beings who entrust themselves—*namu*—we know that the import of the six characters *na-mu-a-mi-da-butsu* is precisely that all of us sentient beings are equally saved. Hence our realization of other-power faith is itself expressed by the six characters *na-mu-a-mi-da-butsu.* We should recognize, therefore, that all the scriptures

805b

have the sole intent of bringing us to entrust ourselves to the six characters *na-mu-a-mi-da-butsu.*

Respectfully.

10. On Faith as Fundamental

What is taught by the Master [Shinran] and by his school is that faith is fundamental. For when we cast away the sundry practices and singleheartedly take refuge in Amida, birth [in the Pure Land] is assured by the Buddha through the inconceivable working of the Vow. [Attaining] this state is also described [in the *Larger Sutra*] as "entering, with the awakening of the one thought-moment [of entrusting], the company of those [whose birth in the Pure Land is] truly settled" (*Daimuryōjukyō*, T.12:272b; *Jōdo ronchū*, T.40:826b; *Kyō-gyōshinshō*, T.83:597b). The nenbutsu, saying the Name of the Buddha, should then be understood as the nenbutsu of gratitude in return for Amida's benevolence, through which the Tathāgata has established our birth.

Respectfully.

11. On the Anniversary [of Master Shinran's Death]

Among those who make the pilgrimage, bring offerings, and come before the [image of] the Master [Shinran] to repay their indebtedness and express their gratitude during this anniversary, there will be those who have realized faith. There will also be those who are lacking in faith (*fushinjin*). This is an extremely serious matter. For unless there is a decisive settling of faith, the birth that is to come in the fulfilled land is uncertain. Therefore, those whose faith is lacking (*fushin*) should in all haste attain the decisive mind.

The human realm is a place of uncertainty. The Land of Utmost Bliss is one of eternity. Hence we should not make our abode in the uncertain human realm, but rather aspire to [birth in] the eternal Land of Utmost Bliss. In our tradition, therefore, the matter of faith is placed before all else; unless we are fully aware of the reason for this, everything is meaningless. We must promptly undergo a decisive settling of faith (*anjin*) and aspire to birth in the Pure Land.

What is widespread in the world and what everyone has in mind is that if they just say the Name with their lips, without any understanding, they will be born in the Land of Utmost Bliss. That is most uncertain. Receiving 805c other-power faith is a matter of fully knowing the import of the six characters *na-mu-a-mi-da-butsu* and thereby undergoing a settling of faith.

As for the substance of faith, [a passage] in the [*Larger*] *Sutra* states: "Hear the Name and realize faith and joy" (*Daimuryōjukyō,* T.12:272b; *Kyō-gyōshinshō,* T.83:601a, 605a). Shandao has said: *"Namu* means 'to take refuge.' It also signifies aspiring to be born and directing virtue. *Amida-butsu* is the practice (*Kangyōsho,* T.37:250ab; *Kyōgyōshinshō,* T.83:594c).

The meaning of the two characters *na-mu* is that we abandon the sundry practices and, without doubting, entrust ourselves singleheartedly and stead-fastly to Amida Buddha. The meaning of the four characters *a-mi-da-butsu* is that, without any effort on our part, [Amida] saves sentient beings who sin-gleheartedly take refuge in him. This is the very essence of the four characters *a-mi-da-butsu.* To understand *namu-amida-butsu* in this way is, therefore, to receive faith. This, in other words, is [the understanding of] the nenbutsu prac-titioner who has fully realized other-power faith.

Respectfully.

12. On the Sleeve [of Amida]

Those who wish to know in full what settled mind means in our tradition need no wisdom or learning at all. For when we simply realize that we are wretched beings of deep evil karma and know that the only buddha who saves even such people as these is Amida Tathāgata, and when, without any 806a contriving but with the thought of holding fast to the sleeve of Amida Buddha, we entrust ourselves [to him] to save us, [bringing us to buddhahood] in the afterlife, then Amida Tathāgata deeply rejoices and, sending forth from himself eighty-four thousand great rays of light, receives us within that light. Hence this is explained in the [*Contemplation*] *Sutra:* "The light shines throughout the worlds of the ten directions and sentient beings mindful of the Buddha are embraced, never to be abandoned" (*Amidakyō,* T.12:343b). This you should know.

There is, then, no anxiety over becoming a buddha. How incomparable is the all-surpassing Primal Vow! And how gracious is Amida Tathāgata's light! Without encountering the [receptive] condition of this light, there can be no cure at all for the fearful sickness of ignorance and karma-hindrance, which has been ours from the beginningless past.

Prompted by the [receptive] condition of this light, and with the ripening of good from the past, we assuredly attain other-power faith now. It is immediately clear, however, that this is faith granted by Amida Tathāgata. Hence we know now, beyond question, that this is not faith generated by the practitioner, but that it is Amida Tathāgata's great other-power faith. Accordingly, all those who have once attained other-power faith should reflect gratefully on Amida Tathāgata's benevolence and repeat the nenbutsu, saying the Name of the Buddha always, in gratitude for the Buddha's benevolence.

Respectfully.   806b

13. On the Unsurpassed,
Most Profound Virtues
and Benefits

Since the phrase *namu-amida-butsu* consists of only six characters, we may not realize that it has such virtue; yet the magnitude of the unsurpassed, most profound virtues and benefits within this Name of six characters is absolutely beyond measure. We should know, therefore, that the realization of faith is contained in these six characters. There is absolutely no faith apart from this or outside of the six characters.

Shandao explains the six characters of this *na-mu-a-mi-da-butsu,* saying (*Kangyōsho,* T.37:250ab; *Kyōgyōshinshō,* T.83:594c):

> *Namu* means "to take refuge." It also signifies aspiring to be born and directing virtue. *Amida-butsu* is the practice. Because of this, we unfailingly attain birth.

How should we understand this explanation?

[The answer is that] if, with [the awakening of] the one thought-moment [of entrusting], a person takes refuge in Amida Buddha—even if his is an existence like ours, burdened with evil karma and blind passions—[Amida], knowing that person, will save him without fail. In other words, "taking refuge" means that we entrust ourselves [to Amida] to save us. [Amida's] bestowal of unsurpassed and great benefit on sentient beings who entrust themselves in the one thought-moment is called "aspiring to be born and directing virtue." Because [Amida] bestows on us sentient beings great goodness and great virtue through [his] "aspiring to be born and directing virtue," the evil karma and blind passions accumulated over myriads of *kalpa*s from the beginningless past are instantly extinguished; hence our blind passions and evil karma all disappear, and we dwell even now in the company of those [whose birth in the Pure Land is] truly settled, in the stage of nonretrogression.

806c

We understand more and more clearly, then, that the six characters *na-mu-a-mi-da-butsu* affirm that we are to be born in the Land of Utmost Bliss. Therefore, one who fully understands the meaning of the six characters of the Name—"settled mind (*anjin*)," or "faith (*shinjin*)"—is said to be a person who has realized great faith given by other-power. Since there is this incomparable teaching, let us deeply entrust ourselves.

Respectfully.

14. On [Women of] Noble and Humble Birth

We must realize that, unbeknownst to others, all women have deep evil karma; whether of noble or humble birth, they are wretched beings. How, then, should they entrust themselves to Amida?

[The answer is that] women who rely firmly and without any anxiety on Amida Tathāgata and accept that [Amida] saves them in [regard to] the most important matter, the afterlife, will unfailingly be saved. If, leaving the depth of their evil to Amida, they simply rely singleheartedly on Amida Tathāgata to save them in [regard to] the afterlife, there is no doubt that [Amida], fully knowing those beings, will save them. Whether there are ten people or one hundred, they need not have the slightest doubt whatsoever that all—each and every one—will be born in the Land of Utmost Bliss. Women who entrust themselves in this way will be born in the Pure Land. They should entrust

807a

themselves ever more deeply to Amida Tathāgata, realizing how shameful it is that until now they have not trusted such an easy path.

Respectfully.

15. On the Primal Vow
of Amida Tathāgata

What sort of sentient beings does the Primal Vow of Amida Tathāgata save? Also, how do we entrust ourselves to Amida, and through what attitude are we saved?

To begin with, in regard to the persons [to be saved], even if they are evil-doers who have committed the ten transgressions and the five grave offenses or women burdened with the five obstacles and the three submissions, they should not be concerned about the depth and weight of their evil karma. It is only by great faith alone, other-power, that we realize birth in the true and real Land of Utmost Bliss.

As for faith, then, what should our attitude be, and how should we entrust ourselves to Amida?

In realizing faith, we simply cast off the sundry practices and disciplines and the evil mind of self-power and, without any doubts, singleheartedly and deeply take refuge in Amida. This we call true and real faith. Amida Tathāgata, fully knowing the sentient beings who singleheartedly and steadfastly entrust themselves in this way, graciously sends forth rays of light, receives these beings within the light, and enables them to be born in the Land of Utmost Bliss. We speak of this as "[Amida's light] embracing sentient beings [who are practitioners] of the nenbutsu."

Beyond this, even though we say the nenbutsu throughout our lives, we should understand that it is the nenbutsu of gratitude for the Buddha's benev-olence. With this, one is to be declared a nenbutsu practitioner who has fully realized our tradition's faith.

Respectfully.   807b

16. On White Bones

When we deeply consider the transiency of this world, [we realize that] what is altogether fleeting is our own span of life: it is like an illusion from beginning to end. And so we have not yet heard of anyone living ten thousand years. A lifetime passes quickly. Can anyone now live to be a hundred? Will I die first, or will my neighbor? Will it be today or tomorrow? We do not know. Those we leave behind and those who go before us are more numerous than the dewdrops that rest briefly beneath the trees and on their leaftips. Hence we may have radiant faces in the morning but in the evening be no more than white bones.

With the coming of the wind of impermanence, both eyes are instantly closed, and when a single breath is forever stilled, the radiant face is drained of life and its vibrant glow is lost. Although family and relatives may gather and grieve broken-heartedly, this is to no avail. As there is nothing else to be done, [the once-familiar form] is taken to an outlying field, and when it has vanished with the midnight smoke, nothing is left but white bones. This is indeed indescribably sad.

And so, because the impermanence of this world creates a condition of uncertainty for young and old alike, we should all immediately take to heart the most important matter, the afterlife, and, deeply entrusting ourselves to Amida Buddha, say the nenbutsu.

Respectfully.

17. On All Women

807c All women—if they are concerned about the afterlife and have a sense of reverence for the buddha-dharma—should simply entrust themselves deeply to Amida Tathāgata, cast off the sundry practices, and rely singleheartedly and firmly [on Amida] to save them [bringing them to buddhahood] in the afterlife. They should have no doubt whatsoever that [such] women will be born without fail in the Land of Utmost Bliss. After they have understood this, then—sleeping or waking—they should just say *Namu-amida-butsu, Namu-amida-butsu,* realizing deeply and wholeheartedly how gracious and wonderful it is that Amida Tathāgata readily receives them within his saving work. We speak of these [women] as people of the nenbutsu who have received faith.

Respectfully.

18. On Master [Shinran]
of Our Tradition

[In realizing] the settled mind expounded by Master [Shinran] of our tradition, we first, without any calculating, cast off our wretchedness and the depth of our evil and dismiss any inclination toward the sundry practices and disciplines; and then, with [the awakening of] the one thought-moment, we entrust ourselves singleheartedly and deeply to Amida Tathāgata to save us, [bringing us to buddhahood] in the afterlife. All those who do this will be saved without exception, ten out of ten, or one hundred out of one hundred. There should not be the slightest doubt about this. Those who fully understand in this way are called "practitioners of faith."

Once [we have realized] this, when we then think of the joy of being saved in the afterlife, we should—sleeping or waking—say *Namu-amida-butsu, Namu-amida-butsu.*

Respectfully.

19. On Evildoers of the
Last [Dharma] Age

Let all evildoers and women of the last [Dharma] age deeply entrust themselves with singleness of mind to Amida Buddha. Apart from that, whatever Dharma they may rely upon, they will never be saved in [regard to] the afterlife.　808a

How, then, should they entrust themselves to Amida Tathāgata, and how should they aspire to the afterlife? They should have no doubt at all that there will unfailingly be deliverance for those who simply rely singleheartedly and firmly on Amida Tathāgata and deeply entrust themselves [to Amida] to save them, [bringing them to buddhahood] in the afterlife.

Respectfully.

20. On Women Attaining
Buddhahood

All women who firmly rely on Amida Tathāgata and entrust themselves [to Amida] to save them in [regard to] the afterlife will unfailingly be delivered.

For Amida Tathāgata himself made the supreme great vow concerning women [who are] abandoned by all [other] buddhas, thinking, "If I do not save women, which of the other buddhas will save them?"

Resolving to go beyond all [other] buddhas and save women, he meditated for five *kalpa*s; undergoing practices for numberless *kalpa*s, he made the all-surpassing great Vow. Thus it is Amida who originated the incomparable vow, "women's attainment of buddhahood." For this reason, women who deeply rely on Amida and entrust themselves [to him] to save them in [regard to] the afterlife will all be born in the Land of Utmost Bliss.

Respectfully.

21. On Passages in the [*Larger*] *Sutra* and in [Tanluan's] Commentary

[The meaning of] settled mind in our tradition [is that] we abandon the inclination toward the sundry practices and disciplines; whatever our evil karma may be (even though it is deep), we leave that to the Buddha and simply, with [the awakening of] the one thought-moment, entrust ourselves single-heartedly and deeply to Amida Tathāgata. Sentient beings who rely on [Amida] to save them will all be delivered, ten out of ten or one hundred out of one hundred. There should not be the slightest doubt whatsoever about this. We speak of those who entrust themselves in this way as people in whom faith (*anjin*) is firmly and rightly settled.

808b

Passages in the [*Larger*] *Sutra* and in [Tanluan's] commentary express this clearly, stating that "with the awakening of the one thought-moment [of entrusting], we dwell in the company of those [whose birth in the Pure Land is] truly settled" (*Daimuryōjukyō*, T.12:272b; *Jōdo ronchū*, T.40:826b; *Kyōgyō-shinshō*, T.83:597b); this refers to "practitioners who have completed the cause [for birth in the Pure Land] in ordinary life." We must, therefore, bear in mind that simply entrusting ourselves deeply to Amida Buddha with [the awakening of] the one thought-moment is of the utmost importance. Other than this, we should say the nenbutsu always—walking or resting, sitting or

134

lying down—realizing the profound benevolence of Amida Tathāgata who readily saves us.

Respectfully.

22. On the Import of Our Tradition's Teaching

Those who seek to know thoroughly the meaning of our tradition's teaching and be born in the Land of Utmost Bliss must first of all know about other-power faith.

What is the essential point of other-power faith? It is the provision by which wretched foolish beings like ourselves go readily to the Pure Land.

In what way does other-power faith find expression? We simply entrust ourselves exclusively to Amida Tathāgata, singleheartedly and steadfastly; and with the awakening of the one thought-moment in which we realize that Amida saves us, Amida Tathāgata unfailingly sends forth his embracing light and keeps us safe within this light as long as we are in this [sahā] world. It is precisely in this state that our birth is assured.

Thus *namu-amida-butsu* expresses the attaining of other-power faith. We must bear in mind that this faith is the source of *namu-amida-butsu*. Then, because we receive this one other-power faith, there is no doubt at all that we will be born readily in the Land of Utmost Bliss. How incomparable is Amida Tathāgata's Primal Vow!

How are we to respond to this gracious benevolence of Amida?

Simply by saying *Namu-amida-butsu,* sleeping or waking, we respond to Amida Tathāgata's benevolence.

With what mind, then, do we say *Namu-amida-butsu?*

Think of it as the rejoicing mind that realizes how gracious and wonderful it is that Amida Tathāgata saves us.

Respectfully.

Shōnyo, disciple of Śākyamuni
(written seal)

808c

Glossary

Ajātaśatru: The son of King Biṃbisāra and Queen Vaidehī, he imprisoned his father and left him to die in jail, thus usurping the throne of Magadha. He also imprisoned his mother. He appears in some sutras as the archetypal evil person who becomes the object of the Buddha's compassion. *See also* Devadatta.

Amida: The Japanese term for Amitābha ("Infinite Light") or Amitāyus ("Infinite Life"). When Dharmākara Bodhisattva fulfilled the Forty-eight Vows he became a buddha by this name and took up residence in his Pure Land in the Western Quarter. The name Infinite Light symbolizes his infinite wisdom, while the name Infinite Life symbolizes his infinite compassion. *See also* Dharmākara; Forty-eight Vows.

Amida Sutra: See three canonical scriptures of the Pure Land school.

Amitābha/Amitāyus. *See* Amida.

anjin: Variously translated as "settled heart," "assurance," "mind-at-rest," and "faith." Although Shinran uses the term on only three occasions, Rennyo, drawing on the *Anjin ketsujōshō,* an important Japanese Pure Land text of uncertain authorship, introduces the concept of *anjin* to interpret Shinran's term for faith, *shinjin. See also* faith; *shinjin.*

apparitional buddha. *See* three bodies of a buddha.

arhat ("one who is worthy of offerings"): One who has eradicated all passions and attained liberation from samsara; the highest stage of spiritual attainment in the Hinayana. *See also* Hinayana; samsara.

bhikṣu: A Buddhist monk.

birth and death: The cycle of birth and death in which sentient beings transmigrate. Due to karmic causes sentient beings are reborn in various realms of existence. *See also* five paths; karma; samsara; six realms of existence; three evil paths.

Buddha ("Awakened One"): Capitalized, the term usually refers to Śākyamuni; in Pure Land texts it often refers to Amida.

buddha-dharma. *See* Dharma.

bodhisattva (lit., "enlightenment being"): One who has engendered the aspiration to attain enlightenment on behalf of all sentient beings; the spiritual ideal of the Mahayana. *See also* Mahayana.

borderland of the Western Paradise: Another name for the transformed Pure Land. The land of imperfect liberation where those who rely on their own abilities and doubt Amida's

137

power are reborn. It is contrasted with the Land of Reward, the sphere of perfect liberation where those with true faith are reborn. *See also* Amida; castle of doubt; Land of Reward; matrix palace; realm of sloth and pride; transformed Pure Land.

calling of the Name. *See* Name; nenbutsu.

castle of doubt: The place of imperfect liberation where those who doubt Amida's power are reborn. *See also* Amida; borderland of the Western Paradise; matrix palace; realm of sloth and pride.

compassion (*jihi*): The word *jihi* consists of two terms: *ji* (Skt. *maitrī*), "affection" or "the desire to give comfort to others"; and *hi* (Skt. *karuṇā*), "pity" or "sympathy for those who suffer and desire to end their suffering." Compassion and wisdom are two of the most important virtues in Mahayana Buddhism. *See also* Mahayana.

compassionate means (Skt. *upāya;* Jp. *hōben*): In Shinshū this term is generally used in one of two ways: to refer to the provisional means (*gonke hōben*) used to lead beings to the truth and reality of the Dharma, or to refer to the compassionate means (*zengyō hōben*) by which the Buddha saves beings through the manifestation of ultimate truth or reality within the world of form and relativity.

compassionate vow. *See* Eighteenth Vow; Original Vow.

completing the cause of birth in ordinary life (*heizei gōjō*): A phrase used by Kakunyo (1270–1351), the third head priest of the Shinshū, in the *Gaijashō;* and also by Zonkaku (1290–1373), the fourth head priest, who explains in the *Jōdo shinyōshō:* "In Master Shinran's school, we teach 'completion of the cause [for birth in the Pure Land] in ordinary life' and do not stress the expectation of birth at life's end. We speak in terms of [Amida's] not coming to meet [the practitioner at the time of death] (a key expectation of followers of earlier Pure Land schools) and do not adhere to the teaching of his coming. . . . If a person encounters the Dharma at the end of his life, then that person is born [in the Pure land] at life's end. We do not speak of [necessarily completing the cause for birth in the Pure Land in] 'ordinary life' or [at] 'life's end'; it is simply that when a person attains faith, he is born, or settled."

Contemplation Sutra: See three canonical scriptures of the Pure Land school.

delusions and attachments (*mōnen mōju*): Mental activity that is a hindrance to enlightenment, which occurs because of the blind passions that are intrinsic to the human condition.

Devadatta: A cousin of Śākyamuni and follower of his teaching. Jealous of the Buddha's authority, he attempted to seize leadership, disrupted the Sangha by raising followers of his own, incited Prince Ajātaśatru to kill his father and usurp the throne of Magadha, and even attempted to kill the Buddha. Because of the gravity of his offenses he is said to have fallen into hell alive.

Dharma: The truth, law; the teachings of the Buddha.

Dharmākara ("Storehouse of the Dharma"): The name of the hero of the *Larger Sutra,* who makes Forty-eight Vows to become a buddha. After long practice he fulfills his vows and becomes Amida Buddha. *See also* Amida; Forty-eight Vows.

diamondlike faith: The steadfast faith, indestructible as a diamond, that is accorded to the devotee by Amida. *See also* Amida; faith; heart of faith.

directing virtue (*ekō*): A concept central to Mahayana teaching, also called transference of merit; it reflects the bodhisattva tradition of undertaking religious practices not only for one's own benefit but also, out of deep compassion, for the sake of all sentient beings. In the path of sages, which encompasses teachings other than those of the Pure Land, *ekō* was interpreted as a practitioner's directing merit toward his own and others' enlightenment. In traditional Pure Land teaching it came to be understood as directing merit toward one's own attainment of birth in the Pure Land, where one would realize enlightenment and then return to this world to work on behalf of all beings. Shinran, however, established an other-power interpretation of *ekō,* in which Amida directs his virtue to practitioners. *See also* bodhisattva; Mahayana; other-power; path of sages.

easy path/practice: Nenbutsu practice or calling the Name of Amida Buddha: *namu amida butsu.* This practice is called "easy" because it enables those of lesser potential to attain rebirth in the Pure Land. It is contrasted with the difficult path, religious practices undertaken by those of greater potential to attain buddhahood in this life. The doctrinal classifications "easy path" and "difficult path" were originally formulated by Nāgārjuna (ca. 150–250) in the "Chapter on Easy Practice" in the *Daśabhūmivibhāṣa-śāstra* (T.26:40–44.) *See also* nenbutsu; Original Vow; path of sages.

eight aspects: The eight main events of the Buddha's life: (1) descending from Tuṣita Heaven, (2) entering his mother's womb, (3) being born, (4) renouncing the world, (5) defeating devils, (6) becoming enlightened, (7) preaching the Dharma, and (8) entering nirvana.

eight difficulties (*hachinan*): The eight circumstances that prevent one from seeing a buddha or hearing the Dharma: (1) existence in hell; (2) existence in the realm of hungry ghosts; (3) existence in the realm of animals; (4) existence in the heaven of long life, where aspiration to enter the Buddhist path does not arise; (5) existence in a remote land: in one of the heavens of the realms of form and formlessness, or in Hokkuru (Uttarakuru), one of the four continents in Buddhist cosmology, where sentient beings are absorbed in pleasures and do not seek the Dharma; (6) being blind, deaf, or mute; (7) being knowledgeable about the world and eloquent; and (8) living in a period before or after a buddha's appearance in the world.

Eighteenth Vow: The vow made by Amida Buddha when he was Dharmākara Bodhisattva: "If, when I attain buddhahood, sentient beings of the ten directions who with sincere mind entrust themselves, aspire to be born in my land, and say my Name perhaps even ten times should not be born there, may I not attain supreme enlightenment. Excluded are those who commit the five grave offenses and those who slander the true Dharma."

eight schools: The eight oldest Japanese Buddhist schools/sects: Kusha, Jōjitsu, Ritsu, Hossō, Sanron, Kegon, Tendai, and Shingon.

enlightenment (Skt. *bodhi*): The state of the highest perfection of wisdom; the state of undefiled purity and eternal bliss.

faith (*shin*): Faith in Amida Buddha. The term *shin* indicates the pure faith transferred by Amida to the devotee, which is distinguished from impure faith that still involves some degree of self-effort. In Shin Buddhism true faith is the only precondition for birth in the Pure Land and is entirely a gift from Amida. Shinran says that when one has true faith one cannot help reciting the nenbutsu, the verbal expression of faith, with a feeling of joy and gratitude. *See also anjin;* heart of faith; nenbutsu.

five defilements (*gojoku*): The five types of defilements prevalent in the last Dharma age: (1) defilements of the age itself, as wars, plagues, and famine increase; (2) defiled views, as evil views spread; (3) defiled passions, as greed, anger, and delusion increase; (4) defiled beings, weakened in mind and body; and (5) a degraded human life span that gradually decreases to ten years. *See also* last Dharma age.

fivefold teachings (*gojū no gi*): The five conditions necessary for birth in the Pure Land: (1) the unfolding of past good; (2) meeting a good teacher; (3) encountering Amida's light; (4) attaining faith; and (5) saying the Name of the Buddha (nenbutsu).

five grave offenses (*gogyaku*): Five acts that normally would cause one to fall into hell: (1) patricide, (2) matricide, (3) killing an arhat (saint), (4) maliciously causing a buddha to bleed, and (5) causing disharmony in the Buddhist Order (sangha).

five obstacles: Buddhist tradition held that a woman faces five obstacles: she cannot become (1) a king of the Brahma Heaven, (2) Indra, (3) a Māra king, (4) a universal monarch (Skt. *cakravartin*), or (5) a buddha.

five paths: The five realms of existence in which sentient beings transmigrate as retribution for evil deeds, the realms of (1) hell, (2) hungry ghosts, (3) animals, (4) human beings, and (5) heavenly beings (Skt. *deva*s). *See also* six realms of existence.

five precepts: Five basic ethical precepts undertaken by all Buddhists: (1) not to kill, (2) not to steal, (3) not to commit adultery, (4) not to lie, and (5) not to take intoxicants.

foolish person: Shin Buddhists self-identify as "foolish people" or "foolish beings" (*bombu*), those who are incapable of performing virtuous actions and are constantly committing evil actions; for these reasons they are the primary objects of Amida's compassion. *See also* virtuous person.

Forty-eight Vows: The vows made by Dharmākara Bodhisattva in the *Larger Sutra,* in which he expressed his desire to create a Pure Land for all sentient beings. *See also* Dharmākara; Eighteenth Vow; Original Vow; Primal Vow; selected Primal Vow; Thirty-fifth Vow.

four modes of birth: The four possible ways that living beings may be born: (1) birth from a womb, (2) birth from an egg, (3) birth from moisture, and (4) birth by metamorphosis.

four peaceful observances: The four Buddhist practices recommended in the *Lotus Sutra* that are disparaged as "self-power" practices in the *Tannishō:* (1) avoiding all people and things that might disturb tranquil meditation, (2) refraining from harmful speech and fault-finding, (3) shunning flattery and sarcasm, and (4) vowing to preach the *Lotus Sutra* to all sentient beings.

fulfilled land (*hōdo*): Shinran taught that within Amida's Pure Land there is a true fulfilled land where the person of true faith (*shinjin*) becomes "one with the light that is the heart of the Tathāgata" at the end of his life; there is also an expedient temporary land where those whose practices are mixed with self-power are born and must remain until they realize faith. *See also* Pure Land.

fushin/fushinjin: Lack of faith. *See also* faith; *shin.*

good teacher (Skt. *kalyāṇamitra*, lit., "good friend"): One who guides people in their spiritual development in the Dharma. *See also* karmically related teacher.

great river of three currents: A river in the realm of the dead that has three currents for three different groups of the dead to cross: (1) a shallow current for those whose sins are shallow, (2) a current with a jeweled bridge for virtuous people, and (3) a current with strong, deep rapids for evildoers.

heart of faith (*shinjin*): *Shinjin* is rendered as the "heart (rather than the "mind") of faith because the heart is the center of the whole being and so comprises not only the intellect but the affective nature as well. *See also* faith.

heaven of the four kings: The first of the six heavens of the realm of desire (*kāmadhātu*), located immediately above the human realm. It is divided into four realms surrounding Mount Sumeru. Its four kings, presiding over the four directions, serve Indra and, like him, protect the Buddhist teaching and its followers.

hell: The lowest of the six realms of existence. *See also* six realms of existence.

hell of incessant pain (Skt. *avīci*): The hottest of the eight scorching hells, where those who have committed the five grave offenses, denied the principle of causality, or slandered the Mahayana suffer unceasing pain.

hell of repeated existence (Skt. *saṃjīva*): The first of the eight great hells, reserved for those who kill living beings.

Hinayana ("Small Vehicle"): A term used by Mahayana Buddhists for various early Buddhist schools whose highest spiritual goal was attainmenr of individual liberation, in contrast to the bodhisattva ideal of the Mahayana. *See also* bodhisattva; Mahayana.

Hōnen (1133–1212): The founder of the Japanese Pure Land (Jōdo) school. Born in Kume in Mimasaka province (present-day Okayama prefecture), at the age of fifteen he went to Mount Hiei where he studied Tendai doctrine under eminent monks. At forty-three, desperately seeking the way to liberation, he discovered the writings of Shandao. After that he considered himself a follower of Shandao and practiced the nenbutsu exclusively. He left Mount Hiei and lived in Yoshimizu, where he propagated the nenbutsu among people from all walks of life. In 1198, at the request of Fujiwara Kanezane, the lord chancellor, he composed the *Senjaku Hongan Nenbutsu Shū* (*Treatise on the Nenbutsu of the Select Original Vow,* T.83:1–20), which marked the founding of the Japanese Pure Land school. In 1206, his school was persecuted by the authorities and he was exiled to Tosa in Shikoku. He died in 1212, a year after he was pardoned and had returned to Kyoto. *See also* Shinran.

Honganji ("Temple of Primal Vow"): The head temple of the Honganji or Ōtani branch of the Shinshū, built by Kakushin-ni, Shinran's daughter, in 1272 as his mausoleum.

The original temple was burned down in 1465 by enemies of the nenbutsu movement. The head temple was rebuilt by Rennyo at Yamashina in Yamashiro province (present-day Kyoto) in 1579.

human realm. *See* five paths; three evil paths; six realms of existence.

ignorance (Skt. *avidyā*): The basic cause of suffering that hinders gaining insight into the Buddha's wisdom. It takes two forms: wrong beliefs and the absence of wisdom. Ignorance, greed, and anger are called "the three poisons."

Ikkōshū ("singleminded school"): A name applied to Shinshū practitioners originating with Ippen (1239–1289), the founder of the Jishū sect. In a letter dated Entoku 2 (1490), Rennyo states that it has been a great mistake for members of the Honganji (as well as others) to refer to their tradition as "Ikkōshū."

Jōdo Shinshū. *See* Shinshū.

Jōdoshū: The Pure Land school, the school founded by Hōnen. *See also* Hōnen.

kalpa: An eon, an immeasurably long period of time. There are four types of *kalpa*s: small, medium, great, and incalculable.

kami: The deities of Shintō, the aboriginal religion of Japan.

karma: Any action of the body, speech, or mind. Since most actions have a good or evil effect on a person's character and determine the nature of his or her future existence, the concept came to be connected with the Buddhist theory of transmigration. *See also* birth and death; passions; samsara.

karmically related teacher: A spiritual mentor in the Buddhist Way, who furthers one's awakening and to whom one is drawn through karmic relations in one's past and present lives. *See also* good teacher.

Kyōgyōshinshō (*Teaching, Practice, Faith, and Enlightenment*): The abridged title of Shinran's major six-fascicle work, *Ken jōdo shinjitsu kyōgyōshō monrui* (*A Collection of Passages Concerning Teaching, Practice, and Attainment That Reveals the Truth of the Pure Land,* T.83:589–644).

Land of Reward: Another name for the Pure Land created by Amida Buddha on fulfilling the Forty-eight Vows. The word "reward" means that it is a reward for his vows and practice. The realm where those who have true faith are reborn. *See also* Amida; Forty-eight Vows; Pure Land.

Land of Supreme Bliss/Land of Utmost Bliss. *See* Pure Land.

Larger Sutra: See three canonical scriptures of the Pure Land school.

last Dharma age (*mappō*): According to Buddhist teachings, the Buddha predicted that after his demise the Dharma would go through three successive stages of degeneration: (1) the period of the true Dharma (*shōbō*), when the Buddha's teaching was practiced and enlightenment could be attained; (2) the period of the semblance Dharma (*zōbō*), when the teaching was practiced but enlightenment was no longer possible; and (3) the last Dharma age (*mappō*), when people are incapable of understanding the Dharma or practicing it.

Lotus Sutra (*Saddharmapuṇḍarīka-sūtra*): One of the most popular and influential Mahayana sutras in China and Japan; the basic text of the Tendai and Nichiren schools. The Mahayana concept of the One Vehicle is a main theme of this text. There are several Chinese translations, of which the version rendered by Kumārajīva in 406 (T.9:1–62) became the most popular. *See also* Mahayana; One Vehicle.

Mahayana ("Great Vehicle"): A form of Buddhism that appeared in India around 100 B.C.E. and which exalted as its religious ideal the bodhisattva, great beings who are willing to forgo their own enlightenment until all sentient beings are liberated. Such selfless compassion becomes possible only when the practitioner grasps the central Mahayana doctrine of *sūnyatā* (emptiness) and so realizes that "self" and "others" are not separate as we usually believe. Mahayanists referred to the early Buddhist teachings as the Hinayana ("Lesser Vehicle)." *See also* bodhisattva; Hinayana.

mappō. See last Dharma age.

matrix palace: A part of the Pure Land in which those of imperfect faith are reborn inside lotus buds, where they remain for several *kalpa*s and can neither see the Buddha nor hear his teaching, until the lotus buds eventually open. *See also* borderland of the Western Paradise; castle of doubt; realm of sloth and pride.

mianjin: A spiritual state in which *anjin* (settled heart or mind) is yet to be realized. *See also anjin;* faith.

Mount Hiei. *See* Nara and Mount Hiei.

Nāgārjuna (ca. 150–250): An important Mahayana philosopher, acknowledged as a founder by eight of the main Mahayana schools in the Buddhist tradition. *See also* eight schools.

Name: The so-called six-character Name of Amida, *na-mu-a-mi-da-butsu* (*namu-amida-butsu*). Recitation of the Name is called the nenbutsu or *shōmyō* ("calling the name"). *See also* Amida; nenbutsu.

Nara and Mount Hiei: Two principal centers of traditional Buddhist learning in the time of Hōnen and Shinran. Nara was the headquarters of earlier sects including the Hossō, Kusha, Ritsu, and Kegon, dating from the Nara period (710–793). Mount Hiei, located between Kyoto and Shiga prefecture, was the monastic center of Tendai Buddhism. In 787 Saichō (767–822), founder of the Tendai school, built the first Tendai temple on the mountain. Thereafter it was one of the main centers of Buddhist learning in Japan. Many Buddhist teachers of the Kamakura period (1185–1332), notably Hōnen, Shinran, Dōgen, Eisai, and Nichiren, studied there.

naturalness (*jinen*): The spontaneous working of Amida's power, which is beyond all human understanding. The person who attains true faith realizes the life of naturalness.

nenbutsu (Skt. *buddha-anusmṛti,* "recollection of a buddha"): Recitation of the Name of Amida Buddha as it is expressed in the six characters *na-mu-a-mi-da-butsu* ("I call on Amida Buddha"). In his Original Vow Dharmākara Bodhisattva vowed to save those of lesser capacity, those who are only capable of meditating on him up to ten times. Shandao interpreted "meditating ten times" to mean "reciting Amida's Name ten times," a practice that could be done by the least capable person. On the basis of Shandao's interpretation, Japanese Pure Land masters such as Hōnen and Shinran developed their doctrines. In the *Kyōgyōshinshō,* Shinran writes: "Saying the Name breaks through all the ignorance of sentient beings and fulfills all their aspirations. Saying the Name is the supreme, true, and excellent right act; the right act is the nenbutsu; the nenbutsu is *namu-amida-butsu; namu-amida-butsu* is right-mindedness." *See also* Amida; Dharmākara; Hōnen; Name; Original Vow; Shandao; Shinran.

Nenbutsubō (also known as Nen Amida Butsu, 1156–1251): A disciple of Hōnen.

nirvana: The stopping or cessation of all passions and desires; the state of liberation, contrasted with samsara. *See also* samsara.

nonretrogression (*futaiten*): Originally this term designated the stage reached by a very advanced bodhisattva who will never retrogress to an inferior state. For Shinran and Rennyo, those who have realized faith have "entered the ocean of Amida's Primal Vow" and so have reached the stage of nonretrogression. *See also* bodhisattva; truly settled.

not waiting for Amida to come to meet us at the moment of death. *See* completing the cause of birth in ordinary life.

one mind (*isshin*): Shinran draws a distinction between the "three minds" of the *Larger Sutra* and the *Contemplation Sutra* and what seemed to be the "one mind" of self-power nenbutsu practice in the *Amida Sutra.* However, he believed that in its unstated but implicit aspect this seemingly counterproductive "one mind" teaching actually reveals the true Dharma leading beings to great faith. *See also* other-power.

oneness of the person [to be saved] and the Dharma [that saves] (*kihō ittai*): In the realization of faith Amida graciously causes his mind and that of a foolish being to become one.

one thought-moment of taking refuge in Amida (*ichinen kimyō*): *Ichinen* has historically encompassed several meanings, including "one moment," "one thought of entrusting," and "one recitation of the nenbutsu." In the *Ichinen tanen mon'i* Shinran links the aspects of time and faith: "One thought-moment is time at its ultimate limit, where realization of *shinjin* (faith) takes place." In the *Kyōgyōshinshō* he explains *kimyō* as follows: "In the term 'to take refuge (*kimyō*),' *ki* means 'to arrive at'; *myō* means 'to act,' 'to invite,' 'to command,' 'to teach,' 'path,' 'message,' 'to devise,' 'to summon.' Thus *kimyō* is the command of the Primal Vow calling to and summoning us." On many occasions Rennyo uses the two terms independently, as in letters I:3 and I:13, respectively; for an expanded example of the terms in combination, see letter IV:1: "With the awakening of the one thought-moment (*ichinen hokki*) in which a practitioner for whom past good has unfolded takes refuge in Amida, the Buddha embraces that practitioner [who has taken refuge through the one thought-moment] with his compassionate light."

One Vehicle (Skt. *ekayāna;* Jp. *ichijō*): The doctrine also known as the buddha vehicle, described in such sutras as the *Lotus Sutra,* by which all sentient beings can attain buddhahood. According to the *Lotus Sutra* the One Vehicle is the ultimate teaching of the Buddha; the Buddha taught three other types of teachings, for *śrāvakas* (Skt., "hearers," early disciples of the Buddha), *pratyekabuddhas* (Skt., "self-enlightened one"), and bodhisattvas, in accordance with their different natures and abilities but did so only as skillful means to ultimately guide all sentient beings to the One Vehicle. In the *Kyōgyōshinshō* Shinran identifies the teaching of the One Vehicle with that of the Eighteenth Vow. *See also* Eighteenth Vow.

Original Vow (Skt. *pūrva-praṇidhāna*): The Forty-eight Vows undertaken by Dharmākara Bodhisattva in the *Larger Sutra,* in which he expressed his desire to create a Pure Land for the liberation of all sentient beings. This term sometimes refers specifically to Dharmākara's Eighteenth Vow: "When I have attained buddhahood, all the sentient beings of the ten directions will be of sincere mind, have serene faith, and wish to be born in my country. If they are not born there even after meditating on me up to ten times, may I not attain perfect enlightenment. Excluded are those who have committed the five criminal acts and abused the right Dharma." *See also* Amida; Dharmākara; Eighteenth Vow; faith; Pure Land.

other-power: The power of Amida's Primal Vow to save all sentient beings. This term is contrasted with self-power or self-effort, religious efforts undertaken by a practitioner relying on his own abilities. The two categories of "other-power" and "self-power" were originally formulated by Tanluan, the third patriarch of Shin Buddhism, in his commentary on Vasubandhu's *Sukhāvatīvyūha-upadeśa* (T.40:844a), as a reformulation of Nāgārjuna's categories of "easy path/practice" and "difficult path/practice," also called the "path of sages." *See also* easy path/practice; path of sages; Primal Vow; Tanluan.

other schools/sects (*tamon/ tashū*): Other branches of the Jōdoshū, such as the Chinzei, Kubon, and Seizan, that acknowledge Hōnen as their founder; sectarian Buddhist movements other than Pure Land schools, such as Tendai, Nichiren, and Zen.

passions (Skt. *kleśa,* "defilement"): Afflictive mental states such as greed, anger, and ignorance that disturb and distress the mind and body and cause one to transmigrate through the cycle of birth and death (samsara). *See also* birth and death.

past good (*shukuzen*): The effect of one's positive karma from the past, including positive karma from one's past lives. Although this term appears only once in Shinran's literary corpus, Rennyo uses the term frequently in the thirteenth chapter of the *Tannishō. See also* karma.

path of sages (*shōdō*): Pure Land teachings divide the Buddhist tradition into two paths: (1) the path of sages, formalized religious practice leading to enlightenment, and (2) the Pure Land (*jōdo*) path, in which one attains rebirth in the Pure Land through the other-power of Amida. These two paths were originally formulated by the Chinese monk Daochuo (Dōshaku, 562–645), regarded as the fourth Pure Land patriarch by Shinran, in the *An luo ji* (T.47:4–22). In Rennyo's usage the term refers to the Tendai, Shingon, and Zen teachings, which were seen as based on self-power practices rather than on other-power practices. *See also* other-power; self-power.

perfection of generosity: The first of the six *pāramitā*s (perfections), or virtues, practiced by a bodhisattva on the path to buddhahood: (1) generosity (Skt. *dāna*), (2) keeping the precepts (Skt. *śīla*), (3) forbearance or patience (Skt. *kṣānti*), (4) effort (Skt. *vīrya*), (5) meditation (Skt. *dhyāna*), and (6) wisdom (Skt. *prajñā*). *See also* bodhisattva; precepts.

period of firm practice of the nenbutsu: The last Dharma age, during which it is said that of all Buddhist practices only the practice of the nenbutsu will be firm. *See also* last Dharma age.

precepts (Skt. *śīla*): Vows concerning moral conduct taken by lay Buddhists and monastics. The five basic precepts to be followed by all Buddhists are: (1) not to kill, (2) not to steal, (3) not to commit adultery, (4) not to lie, and (5) not to take intoxicants. In the Buddhist Order (sangha) there are two hundred and fifty monastic rules for monks and three hundred and forty-eight for nuns.

Primal Vow (Skt. *pūrva-praṇidhāna*): The vows made by a bodhisattva at the outset of his religious career; especially, the Forty-eight Vows undertaken by Dharmākara Bodhisattva to save all sentient beings and establish a Pure Land for them. *See also* Forty-eight Vows; Eighteenth Vow; Original Vow; selected Primal Vow.

Pure Land (Skt. Sukhāvatī, "Land of Bliss"; Jp. Jōdo): The name of the buddha land in the Western quarter, created by Dharmākara Bodhisattva when he fulfilled the Forty-eight Vows and became Amida Buddha. This land symbolizes the sphere of ultimate truth or of perfect peace and happiness. Also called Land of Supreme Bliss or Land of Utmost Bliss.

Pure Land path: The path of practice by which one attains rebirth in the Pure Land through the other-power of Amida Buddha. This path is synonymous with the "easy path/practice" and "other-power," and contrasted with the path of sages, which relies on self-power practices. *See also* Amida; easy path/practice; other-power; path of sages.

realization of no birth and no death: The term "no birth and no death" was often used by Mahayanists to describe the ultimate nature of things. It means that although phenomena appear to originate and perish, when they are seen from the viewpoint of ultimate truth, or *śūnyatā* (Skt., "emptiness"), they do not.

realm of sloth and pride: The land of imperfect liberation where arrogant people are reborn, as such people are self-important and lax in their practice. *See also* borderland of the Western Paradise; castle of doubt; matrix palace.

rebirth in the Pure Land: In the Pure Land tradition practitioners seek rebirth in the Pure Land after death so that they can attain buddhahood there. *See also* Pure Land; Pure Land path.

Rennyo (1414–1499): The eighth abbot of the Honganji, known as the restorer or renewer of the Shin Buddhist tradition. Rennyo often used the name Kenju, which he received at tonsure, and his posthumous name is Shinshō-in. The eldest son of Zonnyo, the seventh abbot of the Honganji, he studied under Keikaku, head of the Hossō sect, and under his own father and grandfather. On many occasions he accompanied his father on preaching tours to places where Shinran had previously taught. On Zonnyo's death in 1457 he became abbot of the Honganji. Partly because of his talent for preaching in simple language, he was able to attract Shinshū followers in towns and villages.

In 1465 jealous priests from Mount Hiei attacked and burned the Honganji, forcing Rennyo to flee to the northeast district of Japan, where he engaged in propagation for some years. In 1471 he founded a temple at Yoshizaki (present-day Fukui prefecture), where he stayed for four years. In 1475, he went to Kawachi province to spread the teachings of Shinran, and in 1478 he restored the Honganji at Yamashina (present-day Kyoto). In 1496 he founded the Ishiyama Honganji, a branch temple of the Honganji, at Ikutama. He died at Yamashina in 1499 at the age of eighty-five. He wrote, among other things, the *Shōshinge taii,* the *Gozokushō,* and over two hundred letters, eighty of which were selected and edited by his grandson Ennyo to form the five-fascicle collection known as the *Ofumi* (*Letters of Rennyo*; T.83:771–808). Rennyo's profound and longlasting impact on Shin teaching is due to these writings, along with the *Goichidaiki kikigaki* (*Records of Rennyo's Talks,* T.83:809–832), a record of his lectures compiled by his disciples.

ri: A unit of measurement for distance, approximately 2.5 miles.

rightly established state: The state attained by the third of three types of people described in the Eighteenth, Nineteenth, and Twentieth of Dharmākara Bodhisattva's Forty-eight Vows. The Nineteenth Vow describes the "wrongly established ones" who rely on their own efforts (self-power) in undertaking various religious practices to achieve rebirth in the Pure Land. The Twentieth Vow describes the "indeterminate ones" who practice the nenbutsu, the practice made possible by Amida's other-power, but who do not have true faith and continue to depend on their own abilities and attain only imperfect liberation. The "rightly established ones," described in the Eighteenth Vow, are those who practice the nenbutsu with true faith in Amida, are in stage of nonretrogression from which they cannot fall back into evil states, and are assured of rebirth in the Pure Land and attainment of buddhahood. *See also* Amida; Dharmākara; Eighteenth Vow; Forty-eight Vows; Original Vow; other-power; Pure Land; self-power; Twnetieth Vow; vow of ultimate deliverance.

right practices (*shōgyō*): The five religious practices that lead to birth in the Pure Land: (1) reciting the Pure Land sutras, (2) contemplating Amida and his land, (3) worshiping Amida, (4) saying the nenbutsu, and (5) praising and making offerings to Amida. Of these, saying the nenbutsu is the act by which rebirth in the Pure Land is truly acomplished; the remaining four are considered auxiliary practices. *See also* sundry practices.

rules of conduct (*okite*): Regulations governing the conduct of Shinshū followers.

sahā (Skt.): The defiled world of samsara; this world. *See also* birth and death; samsara.

Śākyamuni ("sage of the Śākya clan," 565–486 B.C.E.): Born Prince Siddhārtha Gautama in the small kingdom of Kapilavastu in central India, he left his family at the age of twenty-nine to seek the way of liberation. After six years of seeking and arduous practice he attained enlightenment and became the Buddha ("Awakened One"), and traveled throughout northern India teaching the Dharma he had discovered until his death at the age of eighty. His life and teachings form the basis of Buddhism.

same stage as Maitreya: Maitreya Bodhisattva, who resides in Tuṣita Heaven, will appear in this world as its next buddha after 5,670,000,000 years. One who has experienced the settling of faith through the working of Amida is comparable to Maitreya in that both have attained the stage immediately preceding buddhahood.

samsara: Transmigration, the cycle of birth and death. Because of karmic causes sentient beings transmigrate within the six realms of existence. The Buddha's teachings are designed to liberate sentient beings from samsara, which is generally contrasted with nirvana or enlightenment. *See also* birth and death; karma; nirvana; six realms of existence.

sangha: In early Buddhism, the community of ordained Buddhist monks and nuns (the Order). The term was later applied to the entire community of Buddhist devotees, including lay practitioners.

saying the Name. *See* nenbutsu; right practices.

secret teachings: This term applies most directly to esoteric traditions such as Shingon. In medieval Japan, however, a process of esotericization was common to most Buddhist sects, especially the Tendai, whose teachings Shinran found unsatisfactory. Although both Shinran and Rennyo emphatically rejected the idea of secret teachings, they have remained a vexing issue for the Shinshū from Shinran's time until today.

Seikanbō (1182–1238): A disciple of Hōnen, author of the *Senjaku Yōtetsu,* the *Kōgi Zuiketsu-shū,* and other works.

selected Primal Vow (*senjaku hongan*): The term may refer in general to the Forty-eight Vows undertaken by Dharmākara Bodhisattva; it has come to refer specifically to the Eighteenth Vow because that vow singles out the nenbutsu as the cause of birth in the Pure Land. *See also* Dharmākara; Eighteenth Vow; Forty-eight Vows; Primal Vow.

self-power: The religious efforts of a practitioner relying on his own abilities. *See also* other-power.

Shandao (Zendō, 613–681): Fifth of the seven patriarchs of Shin Buddhism, known as the systematizer of Chinese Pure Land doctrine. He was the first explicit advocate of nenbutsu recitation, as opposed to earlier forms of nenbutsu practice that involved meditation on or visualization of Amida. His principal work is the four-volume *Commentary on the Contemplation Sutra* (T.37:245–278). Hōnen became a Pure Land follower after reading this text.

Shin Buddhism. *See* Shinshū.

Shingon: An esoteric Japanese Buddhist school founded by Kūkai (774–835). The term *shingon* (lit., "true word") refers to mantra, words or phrases that have mystic power. *See also* three esoteric practices.

shinjin. See faith; heart of faith.

Shinran (1173–1262): The founder of Shin Buddhism. Born in Kyoto, he was the son of an aristocrat, Hino Arinori. In 1181 he became a monk on Mount Hiei, where he trained in Tendai teachings and practice for ten years. In 1191 he traveled to Kōfukuji in Nara to study. In 1197 he returned to Mount Hiei, where he was in charge of a meditation hall. In 1201 he attempted to meditate in the Rokkakudō Hall for one hundred days;

on the ninety-fifth day he had a vision of Prince Shōtoku. After that, he visited Hōnen, the founder of the Jōdo school, at Yoshimizu. Deeply impressed by Hōnen, he became his follower and started to practice the nenbutsu exclusively. Hōnen gave him the name Shakkū. When he was thirty he again changed his name, to Zenshin, after Avalo-kiteśvara Bodhisattva called him by that name in a dream. In 1207, due to official persecution of the nenbutsu movement, he was exiled to Kokufu in Echigo (present-day Niigata prefecture), stripped of his priestly status, and given a lay name, Fujii Yoshizane. In Echigo he married Eshinni, had children, and renamed himself Gutoku Shinran ("Foolish Bald-headed Shinran"). He was pardoned in 1211 but did not return to Kyoto. In 1214 he moved to the Kantō area (present-day Tokyo area), where he taught the nenbutsu. In 1224 he composed his major work, the *Kyōgyōshinshō,* at Inada. At around the age of sixty, after residing in Hitachi for about twenty years, he returned to Kyoto. There he composed a number of texts, including many *wasan* (Japanese Buddhist hymns). In 1256 he disowned his oldest son, Zenran (1212–1292), for having deceived nenbutsu followers in the Kantō area by claiming falsely that his father had transmitted a secret teaching to him. The resulting confusion prompted some of Shinran's disciples, including Yuienbō (who later composed the *Tannishō*), to visit him in Kyoto and inquire into his views on Buddhism. *See also* Hōnen; Shinshū; Yuienbo.

Shinshū ("true teaching/school"): Also called Jōdo Shinshū or Shin Buddhism. For Shinran the term Jōdo Shinshū meant "true Pure Land teaching" and designated the teachings of Hōnen. After Shinran's death it became the name of the school Shinran founded.

Shōnin: An honorific title used for the founder of a Buddhist school or for an eminent monk; e.g., Shinran Shōnin, Hōnen Shōnin; Rennyo Shōnin.

Shōtoku Taishi (Prince Shōtoku, 574–622): One of the earliest patrons of Buddhism in Japan. Three commentaries (T.56:1–127) on three Mahayana sutras, the *Lotus Sutra,* the *Vimalakīrtinirdeśa-sūtra,* and the *Śrīmāladevīsiṃhanāda-sūtra,* are attributed to him. In 604 he promulgated the first Japanese constitution, the Seventeen-Article Constitution, which was based on Buddhist and Confucian ideals.

singleminded and exclusive practice of the nenbutsu: Shinshū devotional practice. *See also* nenbutsu; Shinshū.

single practice of the nenbutsu and singlemindedness (*senju sennen*): A term that, for Rennyo, reflects complete reliance on other-power. *See also* other-power.

six paths. *See* six realms of existence.

six realms of existence: According to Buddhist teachings all beings transmigrate through six realms in accordance with their karma: (1) the realm of gods (Skt. *deva*s), (2) the realm of angry demigods (Skt. *asura*s), 3) the realm of humans, (4) the realm of animals, (5) the realm of hungry ghosts (Skt. *preta*s), and (6) the hell realm (Skt. *naraka*). Those who commit grave sins fall into hell, where they endure tortuous suffering for a very long time. *See also* five paths; karma; samsara.

six senses: The six physical senses of the eyes, ears, nose, tongue, body, and mind.

skillful means (Skt. *upāya;* Jp. *hōben*): Expedient methods by which buddhas or bodhisattvas, out of compassion, teach sentient beings and guide them to the Dharma.

Smaller Sutra: See three canonical scriptures of the Pure Land school.

stage equal to perfect enlightenment (*tōshōgaku*): For Shinran this term is synonymous with the stage of the truly settled; both terms refer to the spiritual condition of a person who has been embraced by Amida, never to be abandoned.

sundry practices (*zōgyō*): Self-power–oriented good acts apart from the right practices that lead to birth in the Pure Land. *See also* right practices; self-power.

superhuman powers (Skt. *abhijñā*): Various superhuman abilities of buddhas and bodhisattvas, of which the six most notable are: (1) the ability to manifest oneself in any place, (2) the ability to see things at any distance, (3) the ability to hear any sound at any distance, (4) the ability to know the thoughts of others, (5) the ability to know the past lives of oneself and others, and (6) the power to totally eradicate defilements.

sutra(s): Buddhist scriptures that contain the spoken words of the Buddha. One of the three categories of Buddhist literature known as the Tripiṭaka ("three baskets"): Sutra, Vinaya (monastic codes), and Abhidharma (scholastic treatises).

Tanluan (Donran, 476–542): The third of the seven patriarchs of the Shinshū. His main work, the *Ōjōronchū* (T.40:826–843), a commentary on Vasubandhu's *Pure Land Treatise* (*Sukhāvatīvyūha-sūtra-upadeśa,* T.26:230–233), translated into Chinese early in the sixth century by the Indian monk Bodhiruci, provides the basis for the doctrinal systems of Shandao, Shinran, and others. *See also* Shinshū.

Tathāgata: Literally, "one who has gone to (Skt. *gata*) and come from (Skt. *āgata*) the truth of suchness (Skt. *tathā*)," i.e., one who embodies the ultimate truth of suchness (*tathā*); one of the ten epithets of the Buddha. In Pure Land Buddhism it refers to either Amida Buddha or Śākyamuni Buddha.

Tendai (Ch. Tiantai): A school of Mahayana Buddhism founded in China by Chigi (Ch. Zhiyi, 538–597), based on the *Lotus Sutra* and the doctrines of Nāgārjuna. Japanese Tendai was established by Saichō (also known as Dengyō Daishi, 767–822) who brought the Tendai tradition back from China in 805. Saichō later built Enryakuji on Mount Hiei as a center of Tendai study and practice. Japanese Tendai differs from Chinese Tiantai in that it is a doctrinal system consisting of a mixture of Chinese Tiantai teachings, Zen, esoteric teachings, and Mahayana precepts. *See also* Nara and Mount Hiei.

ten directions: The eight cardinal directions plus the zenith and the nadir; the term signifies "in all directions," "everywhere."

ten transgressions (*jūaku*): (1) Killing, (2) stealing, (3) sexual misconduct, (4) lying, (5) divisive speech, (6) harsh speech, (7) idle speech, (8) greed, (9) anger, and 10) holding wrong views. Also called the ten evils.

thanksgiving services (*hōonkō*): Annual services lasting for seven days, ending on the anniversary of Shinran's death (the twenty-eighth day of the eleventh month by the lunar calendar, the sixteenth day of the first month by the solar calendar).

Thirty-fifth Vow: The thirty-fifth of the Forty-eight Vows undertaken by Dharmākara Bodhisattva when he became Amida Buddha: "If, when I attain buddhahood, those women in the innumerable and inconceivable buddha lands of the ten directions who, hearing my Name, rejoice and entrust themselves, awaken the aspiration for enlightenment, and despise their female bodies should after death again take female form, may I not attain supreme enlightenment." *See also* Amida; Dharmākara; Forty-eight Vows.

thirty-two major marks and eighty minor marks: The physical signs or marks that distinguish the body of a buddha or universal monarch (Skt. *cakravartin*), such as a protuberance on the crown of the head, a curling white hair between the eyebrows, a golden complexion, a long, broad tongue, and an excellent voice.

three acts: Acts of body, speech, and mind.

three bodies of a buddha: (1) The dharma body (Skt. *dharmakāya*), or ultimate truth. (2) The spiritual body or reward body (Skt. *saṃbhogakāya*), a symbolic personification of the dharma body that, as a reward for eons of ascetic practice, a buddha assumes as a skillful means of expounding the Dharma to bodhisattvas and others reborn in his Pure Land. This buddha body always resides in a pure land, e.g., Amida Buddha. (3) The apparitional or transformation body (Skt. *nirmāṇakāya*), an "incarnate" or "historically manifested" body of a buddha that appears in the world to guide sentient beings in a manner adapted to their situations and abilities, e.g., Śākyamuni Buddha.

three canonical scriptures of the Pure Land school: (1) The *Larger Sutra* (Skt. *Sukhā-vatīvyūha-sūtra;* Ch. *Wuliangshou jing;* Jp. *Muryō ju kyō*), of which there are five extant Chinese translations. The translation done by Sanghavarman (T.12:265–279) in 252 became one of the three canonical scriptures of the Pure Land school. Shinran considered this text to be the basis of his Buddhist views. (2) The *Contemplation Sutra* (Skt. *Amitāyurdhyāna-sūtra;* Ch. *Guan wuliangshou fo jing;* Jp. *Kanmuryō ju kyō*): the Chinese translation of this text (T.12:340–346) is attributed to Kalayaśas, a monk from Central Asia, who came to China during the Yuanjia period (424–453). (3) The *Amida Sutra* or *Smaller Sutra* (Skt. *Sukhāvatīvyūha-sūtra;* Ch. *Amituo jing;* Jp. *Amida kyō*), of which there are two Chinese translations. The translation done by Kumārajīva (T.12:346–348) around 402 during the Yao-Qin period became one of the three canonical scriptures of the Pure Land school.

three esoteric practices: Three mystic practices of (1) body (Skt. *mudrā*), meaning physical expressions (usually hand gestures) of mystic signs; (2) speech (mantra), the recitation of magical words, and (3) mind (Skt. *samādhi*), meditation on a buddha or bodhisattva. According to esoteric Buddhist traditions, such as Shingon, when the three esoteric practices of a buddha and those of a practitioner are united the practitioner realizes buddhahood in this life. *See also* Shingon.

three evil paths (*sanzu*): The three evil realms in which sentient beings transmigrate as retribution for evil deeds; the three lowest of the six realms of existence: the realms of (1) hell, (2) hungry ghosts, and (3) animals. *See also* five paths; six realms of existence.

threefold entrusting (*sanshin*): Shinran's interpretation of the Eighteenth Vow, in which the "three minds"—sincere mind (*shishin*), entrusting (*shingyō*), and aspiring to be born in the Pure Land through reliance on other-power (*yokushō*)—together comprise the threefold entrusting, or the three aspects of faith. *See also* Eighteenth Vow; faith.

three minds (*sanjin*): The three types of minds or mental states mentioned in the *Contemplation Sutra:* sincere mind (*shijōshin*), deep mind (*jinshin*), and the mind aspiring to birth in the Pure Land by the transfer of merit (*ekō hotsuganshin*). *See also* threefold entrusting.

three submissions: In Chinese Confucian tradition a woman is expected to submit to the authority of her father, husband, and son.

Tract on Faith Alone (*Yuishinshō*): A text composed by Seikaku (1176–1235), one of Hōnen's disciples. Shinran regarded this text highly and recommended that his followers study it.

transference of merit (Skt. *pariṇāma;* Jp. *ekō*): There is considerable difference between the Shinshū and other Buddhist traditions in their interpretation of this term. In Shinshū, sentient beings' salvation depends totally on the merit that Amida transfers to them, not on merit that they themselves accumulate. In the view of other Buddhist traditions, sentient beings can attain enlightenment through the merit they have accumulated.

transformed Pure Land: The third of the following three buddha lands: (1) the true land, land of ultimate truth; (2) the Land of Reward; and (3) the transformed Pure Land, where nenbutsu practitioners who doubt other-power are born.

truly settled: A term describing those whose birth in the Pure Land is settled (*shōjōju*); such people practice the nenbutsu with true faith in Amida. They are in the stage of nonretrogression from which they are assured of birth in the Pure Land and attainment of buddhahood, as described in the Eighteenth Vow of Dharmākara Bodhisattva. Shinran writes in the *Kyōgyōshinshō:* "When foolish beings possessed of blind passions, the multitudes caught in birth and death and defiled by evil karma, realize the mind and practice that Amida directs to them for their going forth, they immediately join the truly settled of the Mahayana. Because they dwell among the truly settled, they necessarily attain nirvana."

turning of the mind (*eshin*): A term that describes the shift of mind or attitude from relying on one's own self-power to entrusting in the other-power of Amida.

two benefits (*niyaku*): (1) Attaining true faith and joining the ranks of the truly settled, and (2) realizing nirvana, or enlightenment, at death. This is contrasted with the teaching of the one benefit, which equates the attainment of true faith with enlightenment itself.

ultimate truth (Skt. *tathatā*): The truth that is formless, indescribable, and inconceivable. *See also* realization of no birth and death.

Vasubandhu (Seshin or Tenjin, ca. 300–400): The second of the seven patriarchs of the Shinshū and the author of works on the Abhidharma and Yogācāra teachings. His

Pure Land Treatise (T.26:230–233), a commentary on the *Larger Sutra,* became one of the basic texts of the Pure Land tradition in China and Japan.

virtuous person: One who considers himself good or capable of performing virtuous actions, as opposed to followers of Shin Buddhism, who believe themselves to be "foolish people" who are the primary objects of Amida's compassion. *See also* foolish person.

vow (Skt. *praṇidhāna*): At the outset of practice a bodhisattva makes vows to attain enlightenment. *See also* Original Vow.

vow of ultimate deliverance: The Twentieth of the Forty-eight Vows made by Dharmākara Bodhisattva, in which he says that those sentient beings who, having heard his Name, desire to be born in his land and sincerely turn their merit toward that goal shall be born there. Shinran believed that although the sentient beings described in the Twentieth Vow still depend upon their own abilities and doubt Amida's other-power, they will eventually attain rebirth in the Pure Land because Amida promised to accomplish their salvation in the Twentieth Vow. *See also* Amida; Dharmākara; Forty-eight Vows.

wisdom (*prajñā*): Transcendental wisdom. Wisdom and compassion are the two most important virtues in Mahayana Buddhism; a buddha is one who has perfected these two virtues.

Yuienbō (1223–1290): A disciple of Shinran and author of the *Tannishō.* Originally from Hitachi province (present-day Ibaragi prefecture), his lay name was Heijirō. After becoming Shinran's disciple he built a temple at Kawada in Hitachi province. He composed the *Tannishō* about thirty years after Shinran's death.

Zenshin: One of Shinran's names.

Bibliography

Bloom, Alfred. *"Tannisho:* Notes Lamenting the Differences," in *Strategies for Modern Living: A Commentary with the Text of the Tannisho,* pp. 1–23. Berkeley: Numata Center for Buddhist Translation and Research, 1992.

Buddhist Churches of America, ed. "Notes Lamenting Differences (*Tanni Shō*)," in *Shinshu Seiten: Jodo Shin Buddhist Teaching,* pp. 239–268. San Francisco: Buddhist Churches of America, 1978.

——. "The Epistles (*Gobun Shō*)," in *Shinshū Seiten: Jōdo Shin Buddhist Teaching,* pp. 269–390. San Francisco: Buddhist Churches of America, 1978.

Chevrier, Jōdo André, trans. *Tannishō, Notes Deplorant les Differences.* Gstaad: Les Éditions de la Voie Simple, 1980.

Haas, Hans, trans. "Tan-i-shô, Klage über die Häresien, von Nyoshin Shônin," in *Amida Buddha unsere Zuflücht: Urkunden zum Verständnis japanischen Sukhāvatī-Buddhismus,* pp. 129–142. Gōttingen: Vandenhoeck and Ruprecht, 1910.

Hirota, Dennis, trans. *Tannishō, A Primer.* Kyoto: Ryūkoku University, 1982.

Ikeyama, Eikichi, trans. *Tannischo: Das Büchlein vom Bedauern des Abweichenden Glaubens.* Tokyo: Risosha, 1965.

Imadate, Tosui, trans. *The Tannishō, Tract on Deploring the Heterodoxies: An Important Textbook of Shin Buddhism founded by Shinran (1173–1262).* Kyoto: Eastern Buddhist Society, 1928, 1939.

Inagaki, Saizō, trans. *Shinran-Shōnin's Tannishō with Buddhist Psalms.* Nishinomiya, 1949.

Izumoji, Osamu. *Ofumi.* Tōyō Bunko, No. 345. Tokyo: Heibonsha, 1978.

Fujimoto, Ryūkyō, trans. *The Tannishō: A Religion Beyond Good and Evil.* Kyoto: Honpa Hongwanji, 1932, 1955.

Fujiwara, Ryōsetsu, trans. *The Tanni Shō: Notes Lamenting Differences.* Ryūkoku Translation Series II. Kyoto: Ryūkoku University, 1962, 1980.

Goncalves, Prof. Dr. Ricardo Mario, trans. *Tannishō: O Tratado de Lamentacao das Heresias.* Sao Paulo: Templo Budista Higashi-Honganji, 1974.

Okochi, Ryogi, and Klaus Otte, trans. *Tan-ni-shō: Die Gunst des reinen Landes.* Bern: Origo Verlag, 1977.

Oshiro, Kosaburo, trans. *Tannisho, Notas sobre Iamtaciones de las herejias.* Kyoto: Honpa Hongwangi, 1982.

Ōtani, Kōshō, et al., trans. *Tannishō: A Tract Deploring Heresies of Faith*. Kyoto: Higashi Honganji, 1961.

Renondeau, Gaston, trans. "Tannishō," in *Le bouddihisme japonais*. Paris: Editions Albin Michel, 1963.

Ri, Chikō, trans. *Tannishō kaisetsu: Shinkō no sezui*. Seoul: Chōsen Jikei Kyōkai, 1928.

Sakurazawa, Nyoiti (Nyoichi) (Georges Ohsawa), trans. "Tannisyo (regrets de la croyance étrangères), Paroles de Sinran rapportées par son disciple," in *Principe unique de la philosophie et de la science d'Extrême-Orient*, pp. 125–155. Paris: Vrin, 1931, 1973.

Sato, Michio, trans. *Tannishō: Das Büchlein vom Bedauern des Abweichenden Glaubens*. Kyoto: Honpa Honganji, 1977.

Sugi, Shirō. *Gobunshō kōwa*. Kyoto: Nagata Bunshōdō, 1933, 1979.

Sugihira, Shizutoshi. "Rennyo Shōnin, Great Teacher of Shin Buddhism," *The Eastern Buddhist* 8 (May 1949): 5–35.

Suzuki, Daisetz Teitarō. "Rennyo's Letters [V: 5]," in *Mysticism: Christian and Buddhist*, pp. 126–131. New York: Harper and Brothers, 1957.

—. "The Tannishō," in *Collected Writings on Shin Buddhism*, pp. 191–222. Kyoto: Shin-shū-Ōtaniha, 1973.

Tannishō. San Francisco: Asoka Society, 1961.

Troup, James, trans. "The Gobunsho, or Ofumi, of Rennyo Shonin," *Transactions of the Asiatic Society of Japan* 17 (1889): 101–143.

Unno, Taitetsu, trans. *Tannishō, A Shin Buddhist Classic*. Honolulu: Buddhist Study Center Press, 1984

—. *Tannishō: Lamenting the Deviations*. Honolulu: Buddhist Study Center, 1977.

Yamada, Osamu, trans. *Tanni-Shō: Sur le Regret de l'Alteration de la Vraie Croyance*. Geneve: Societe Bouddhique Suisse Jodo-Shin, 1971.

Yamamoto, Kōshō, trans. "The Gobunsho: The Epistles—Extracts," in *The Shinshu Seiten: The Holy Scripture of Shinshu*, pp. 287–298. Honolulu: Honpa Hongwanji Mission of Hawaii, 1955.

—. "The Tannisho: A Book Deploring the Heterodoxies," in *The Shinshu Seiten: The Holy Scripture of Shinshu*, pp. 263–281. Honolulu: Honpa Hongwanji Mission of Hawaii, 1955.

Yokogawa, Kensho. Letters II:4 and V:12 in "Shin Buddhism as the Religion of Hearing," *The Eastern Buddhist* 7 (July 1939): 336–339.

Index

A

act(s), 46, 88
  of devotion, 104
  evil/of treachery, 578, 102
  miscellaneous good, 83–84, 86, 98
  three, of Amida/Buddha, 87, 88
  See also deed(s); karma/karmic
afterlife, 18, 51, 52, 67, 83, 114, 118, 121,
  122, 124, 125, 126, 130, 132, 133, 134
  birth (in the Pure Land), 52, 53, 66, 72,
  94, 98, 101, 116
  buddhahood/enlightenment in, 36, 37,
  50, 62, 74, 81, 95, 114, 115, 117,
  122, 126, 128, 132, 133
age:
  evil future, 103
  present, 67, 114
  See also last Dharma age
Ajātaśatru, 102, 103
Amida, 10, 12–14, 21, 23–25, 33, 37,
  43–45, 48–49, 52, 53, 55–57, 59, 61,
  63, 68–70, 72–74, 76, 77, 79–80,
  84–89, 93, 95, 112–115, 121122,
  124–126, 128–132, 135
  beneficence/benevolence/compassion/
  compassionate means/favor of, 22,
  25, 43, 46, 47, 49, 52, 54, 57, 59, 60,
  61, 69, 71, 75, 76, 77, 80, 81, 82, 88,
  90, 94, 99, 104, 105, 125, 127, 129,
  133
  embrace/embracing, 50, 61, 65, 67, 77,
  79, 89
  entrusting to/reliance on/taking refuge
  in, 36, 37, 42, 48, 49, 52, 55, 57, 59,
  61, 63, 64, 67–72, 73, 76, 77, 79–89,
  93, 98–100, 101, 104, 107, 112,
  114–118, 121–135
  enlightenment, 54, 72, 89
  faith called forth/granted/transferred
  by, 5, 12, 75, 129
  fulfilled land of, 43, 69, 71, 122
  gratitude/indebtedness toward, 12, 20,
  43, 46, 47, 52, 55, 57, 71, 77, 98, 99
  light of, 21, 65, 67, 69, 71, 73, 74–77,
  79, 81, 84–86, 94, 128, 129, 131,
  135
  mind of, 36, 107, 123, 126
  meeting at the moment of death, not
  waiting for, 43–46
  other-power, 33, 63, 75, 76, 80, 82, 98,
  102, 104, 129
  power(s), 11, 18
  vow(s)/Vow, 11, 13, 14, 20, 44, 52, 57,
  59, 65, 82, 84, 93, 95, 102, 122,
  124, 134
  See also Buddha; Dharmākara; Name;
  Vow(s); Pure Land; Tathāgata
a-mi-da/a-mi-da-butsu/Amida-butsu, 77,
  81, 85, 86, 88, 112, 117, 118, 126,
  128, 129
  See also characters, four, three; Name
Amitābha. *See* Amida
anjin, 35–36, 51, 62, 65, 67, 76, 81, 88,
  95, 99, 106, 109, 110, 111, 116, 127,
  130, 134

BDK English Tripiṭaka
(First Series)

Abbreviations

Ch.:   Chinese
Skt.: Sanskrit
Jp.:   Japanese
Eng.: Published title

Title	Taishō No.
Ch. Chang ahan jing (長阿含經) Skt. Dīrghāgama	1
Ch. Zhong ahan jing (中阿含經) Skt. Madhyamāgama	26
Ch. Dasheng bensheng xindi guan jing (大乘本生心地觀經)	159
Ch. Fo suoxing zan (佛所行讚) Skt. Buddhacarita	192
Ch. Zabao zang jing (雜寶藏經) Eng. *The Storehouse of Sundry Valuables* (1994)	203
Ch. Faju piyu jing (法句譬喩經)	211
Ch. Xiaopin banruo boluomi jing (小品般若波羅蜜經) Skt. Aṣṭasāhasrikā-prajñāpāramitā-sūtra	227
Ch. Jingang banruo boluomi jing (金剛般若波羅蜜經) Skt. Vajracchedikā-prajñāpāramitā-sūtra	235
Ch. Daluo jingang bukong zhenshi sanmoye jing (大樂金剛不空眞實三麼耶經) Skt. Adhyardhaśatikā-prajñāpāramitā-sūtra	243
Ch. Renwang banruo boluomi jing (仁王般若波羅蜜經) Skt. *Kāruṇikārājā-prajñāpāramitā-sūtra	245

Title	Taishō No.
Ch. Banruo boluomiduo xin jing (般若波羅蜜多心經) Skt. Prajñāpāramitāhṛdaya-sūtra	251
Ch. Miaofa lianhua jing (妙法蓮華經) Skt. Saddharmapuṇḍarīka-sūtra Eng. *The Lotus Sutra*	262
Ch. Wuliangyi jing (無量義經)	276
Ch. Guan Puxian pusa xingfa jing (觀普賢菩薩行法經)	277
Ch. Dafangguang fo huayan jing (大方廣佛華嚴經) Skt. Avataṃsaka-sūtra	278
Ch. Shengman shizihou yisheng defang bianfang guang jing (勝鬘師子吼一乘大方便方廣經) Skt. Śrīmālādevīsiṃhanāda-sūtra	353
Ch. Wuliangshou jing (無量壽經) Skt. Sukhāvatīvyūha	360
Ch. Guan wuliangshou fo jing (觀無量壽佛經) Skt. *Amitāyurdhyāna-sūtra	365
Ch. Amituo jing (阿彌陀經) Skt. Sukhāvatīvyūha	366
Ch. Da banniepan jing (大般涅槃經) Skt. Mahāparinirvāṇa-sūtra	374
Ch. Fochuibo niepan lüeshuo jiaojie jing (佛垂般涅槃略説教誡經)	389
Ch. Dizang pusa benyuan jing (地藏菩薩本願經) Skt. *Kṣitigarbhapraṇidhāna-sūtra	412
Ch. Banzhou sanmei jing (般舟三昧經) Skt. Pratyutpannabuddhasammukhāvasthitasamādhi-sūtra	418
Ch. Yaoshi liuli guang rulai benyuan gongde jing (藥師琉璃光如來本願功德經) Skt. Bhaiṣajyaguru-vaiḍūrya-prabhāsa-pūrvapraṇidhāna-viśeṣavistara	450
Ch. Mile xiasheng chengfo jing (彌勒下生成佛經) Skt. *Maitreyavyākaraṇa	454
Ch. Wenshushili wen jing (文殊師利問經) Skt. *Mañjuśrīparipṛcchā	468

Title	Taishō No.
Ch. Mohe sengqi lü (摩訶僧祇律) Skt. *Mahāsāṃghika-vinaya	1425
Ch. Sifen lü (四分律) Skt. *Dharmaguptaka-vinaya	1428
Ch. Shanjianlü piposha (善見律毘婆沙) Pāli Samantapāsādikā	1462
Ch. Fanwang jing (梵網經) Skt. *Brahmajāla-sūtra	1484
Ch. Youposaijie jing (優婆塞戒經) Skt. Upāsakaśīla-sūtra Eng. *The Sutra on Upāsaka Precepts*	1488
Ch. Miaofa lianhua jing youbotishe (妙法蓮華經憂波提舍) Skt. Saddharmapuṇḍarīka-upadeśa	1519
Ch. Shizha biposha lun (十住毘婆沙論) Skt. *Daśabhūmika-vibhāṣā	1521
Ch. Fodijing lun (佛地經論) Skt. *Buddhabhūmisūtra-śāstra	1530
Ch. Apidamojushe lun (阿毘達磨俱舍論) Skt. Abhidharmakośa-bhāṣya	1558
Ch. Zhonglun (中論) Skt. Madhyamaka-śāstra	1564
Ch. Yüqie shidilun (瑜伽師地論) Skt. Yogācārabhūmi-śāstra	1579
Ch. Cheng weishi lun (成唯識論)	1585
Ch. Weishi sanshilun song (唯識三十論頌) Skt. Triṃśikā	1586
Ch. Weishi ershi lun (唯識二十論) Skt. Viṃśatikā	1590
Ch. She dasheng lun (攝大乘論) Skt. Mahāyānasaṃgraha Eng. *The Summary of the Great Vehicle*	1593

Title	Taishō No.
Ch. Bian zhongbian lun (辯中邊論) Skt. Madhyāntavibhāga	1600
Ch. Dasheng zhuangyanjing lun (大乘莊嚴經論) Skt. Mahāyānasūtrālaṃkāra	1604
Ch. Dasheng chengye lun (大乘成業論) Skt. Karmasiddhiprakaraṇa	1609
Ch. Jiujing yisheng baoxing lun (究竟一乘寶性論) Skt. Ratnagotravibhāga-mahāyānottaratantra-śāstra	1611
Ch. Yinming ruzheng li lun (因明入正理論) Skt. Nyāyapraveśa	1630
Ch. Dasheng ji pusa xue lun (大乘集菩薩學論) Skt. Śikṣāsamuccaya	1636
Ch. Jingangzhen lun (金剛針論) Skt. Vajrasūcī	1642
Ch. Zhang suozhi lun (彰所知論)	1645
Ch. Putixing jing (菩提行經) Skt. Bodhicaryāvatāra	1662
Ch. Jingangding yuqie zhongfa anouduoluo sanmiao sanputi xin lun (金剛頂瑜伽中發阿耨多羅三藐三菩提心論)	1665
Ch. Dasheng qixin lun (大乘起信論) Skt. *Mahāyānaśraddhotpāda-śāstra	1666
Ch. Shimoheyan lun (釋摩訶衍論)	1668
Ch. Naxian biqiu jing (那先比丘經) Pāli Milindapañhā	1670
Ch. Banruo boluomiduo xin jing yuzan (般若波羅蜜多心經幽贊)	1710
Ch. Miaofalianhua jing xuanyi (妙法蓮華經玄義)	1716
Ch. Guan wuliangshou fo jing shu (觀無量壽佛經疏)	1753
Ch. Sanlun xuanyi (三論玄義)	1852
Ch. Dasheng xuan lun (大乘玄論)	1853
Ch. Zhao lun (肇論)	1858

Title		Taishō No.
Ch.	Huayan yisheng jiaoyi fenqi zhang (華嚴一乘教義分齊章)	1866
Ch.	Yuanren lun (原人論)	1886
Ch.	Mohe zhiguan (摩訶止觀)	1911
Ch.	Xiuxi zhiguan zuochan fayao (修習止觀坐禪法要)	1915
Ch.	Tiantai sijiao yi (天台四教儀)	1931
Ch.	Guoqing bai lu (國清百録)	1934
Ch.	Zhenzhou Linji Huizhao chanshi wulu (鎮州臨濟慧照禪師語録)	1985
Ch.	Foguo Yuanwu chanshi biyan lu (佛果圜悟禪師碧巖録)	2003
Ch.	Wumen guan (無門關)	2005
Ch.	Liuzu dashi fabao tan jing (六祖大師法寶壇經)	2008
Ch.	Xinxin ming (信心銘)	2010
Ch.	Huangboshan Duanji chanshi chuanxin fayao (黃檗山斷際禪師傳心法要)	2012A
Ch.	Yongjia Zhengdao ge (永嘉證道歌)	2014
Ch.	Chixiu Baizhang qinggui (勅修百丈清規)	2025
Ch. Skt.	Yibuzonglun lun (異部宗輪論) Samayabhedoparacanacakra	2031
Ch. Skt. Eng.	Ayuwang jing (阿育王經) Aśokāvadāna *The Biographical Scripture of King Aśoka* (1993)	2043
Ch.	Maming pusa zhuan (馬鳴菩薩傳)	2046
Ch.	Longshu pusa zhuan (龍樹菩薩傳)	2047
Ch.	Posoupandou fashi zhuan (婆藪槃豆法師傳)	2049
Ch. Eng.	Datang Daciensi Zanzang fashi zhuan (大唐大慈恩寺三藏法師傳) *A Biography of the Tripiṭaka Master of the Great Ci'en Monastery of the Great Tang Dynasty* (1995)	2053
Ch.	Gaoseng zhuan (高僧傳)	2059
Ch.	Biqiuni zhuan (比丘尼傳)	2063

Title	Taishō No.
Ch. Gaoseng Faxian zhuan (高僧法顯傳)	2085
Ch. Datang xiyu ji (大唐西域記)	2087
Ch. Youfangjichao: Tangdaheshangdongzheng zhuan (遊方記抄: 唐大和上東征傳)	2089-(7)
Ch. Hongming ji (弘明集)	2102
Ch. Fayuan zhulin (法苑珠林)	2122
Ch. Nanhai jigui neifa zhuan (南海寄歸内法傳)	2125
Ch. Fanyu zaming (梵語雜名)	2135
Jp. Shōmangyō gisho (勝鬘經義疏)	2185
Jp. Yuimakyō gisho (維摩經義疏)	2186
Jp. Hokke gisho (法華義疏)	2187
Jp. Hannya shingyō hiken (般若心經秘鍵)	2203
Jp. Daijō hossō kenjin shō (大乘法相研神章)	2309
Jp. Kanjin kakumu shō (觀心覺夢鈔)	2312
Jp. Risshū kōyō (律宗綱要) Eng. *The Essentials of the Vinaya Tradition* (1995)	2348
Jp. Tendai hokke shūgi shū (天台法華宗義集) Eng. *The Collected Teachings of the Tendai Lotus School* (1995)	2366
Jp. Kenkairon (顯戒論)	2376
Jp. Sange gakushō shiki　(山家學生式)	2377
Jp. Hizōhōyaku (秘藏寶鑰)	2426
Jp. Benkenmitsu nikyō ron　(辨顯密二教論)	2427
Jp. Sokushin jōbutsu gi (即身成佛義)	2428
Jp. Shōji jissōgi (聲字實相義)	2429
Jp. Unjigi (吽字義)	2430
Jp. Gorin kuji myōhimitsu shaku (五輪九字明秘密釋)	2514
Jp. Mitsugonin hotsuro sange mon (密嚴院發露懺悔文)	2527

Title	Taishō No.
Jp. Kōzen gokoku ron (興禪護國論)	2543
Jp. Fukan zazengi (普勧坐禪儀)	2580
Jp. Shōbōgenzō (正法眼藏)	2582
Jp. Zazen yōjin ki (坐禪用心記)	2586
Jp. Senchaku hongan nembutsu shū (選擇本願念佛集)	2608
Jp. Kenjōdo shinjitsu kyōgyō shōmon rui (顯淨土眞實教行証文類)	2646
Jp. Tannishō (歎異抄) Eng. *Tannishō: Passages Deploring Deviations of Faith* (1996)	2661
Jp. Rennyo shōnin ofumi (蓮如上人御文) Eng. *Rennyo Shōnin Ofumi: The Letters of Rennyo* (1996)	2668
Jp. Ōjōyōshū (往生要集)	2682
Jp. Risshō ankoku ron (立正安國論)	2688
Jp. Kaimokushō (開目抄)	2689
Jp. Kanjin honzon shō (觀心本尊抄)	2692
Ch. Fumu enzhong jing (父母恩重經)	2887
Jp. Hasshūkōyō (八宗綱要) Eng. *The Essentials of the Eight Traditions* (1994)	extracanonical
Jp. Sangō shīki (三教指帰)	extracanonical
Jp. Mappō tōmyō ki (末法燈明記) Eng. *The Candle of the Latter Dharma* (1994)	extracanonical
Jp. Jūshichijō kenpō (十七條憲法)	extracanonical